Grandpa's Words of Wisdom

Where You Are, Where You're Heading, And What To Do About It

Stephen L. DeFelice, M.D.

authorHOUSE

AuthorHouse™
1663 Liberty Drive
Bloomington, IN 47403
www.authorhouse.com
Phone: 833-262-8899

Published by AuthorHouse 06/03/2021

ISBN: 978-1-5462-5011-1 (sc)
ISBN: 978-1-5462-5010-4 (e)
ISBN: 978-1-5462-5188-0 (hc)

Library of Congress Control Number: 2018907991

This book is dedicated to

My grandchildren, Olivia and Stephen Carlos DeFelice: Something to ponder upon to guide you in these increasingly complex times.

To your parents, Stephen Francis DeFelice and Norma DeDios DeFelice, who brought you into this world and how lucky you are that you've been showered with their love and guidance.

To Grandma Patrice DeFelice and Grandma Julia DeDios who carried your father and mother in their wombs and brought you into this world.

Acknowledgement

To Patricia Park, my multi-decade friend and colleague whose exceptional intelligence, good spirit and input on each page were instrumental in bringing about the completion of this book. There, however, was one page she refused to review. It dealt with Vlad, The Impaler!

About the Author

As a young physician, Dr. DeFelice became concerned about our lack of medical cures despite our impressive technology. During the Vietnam War he was stationed at WRAIR, the Walter Reed Army Institute of Research, as Chief of Clinical Pharmacology responsible for designing and supervising clinical studies for potential new therapies against malaria and radiation fallout in order to protect our troops. During this period buildings in our Capitol were set to the torch by protesters. He became concerned with that sudden eruption of civil unrest and its escalation up to current times.

While at WRAIR, the Pentagon was the organization first developing the computer which led to the worldwide Internet. Then, over time, he made an alarming observation. The more the worldwide Internet was expanding the more destabilization and destruction of our traditional culture was taking place being supplanted by our technological one. He attributes much of its cause to what he calls the *Internet Democracy*.

Dr. DeFelice studied as a National Institutes of Health fellow in Endocrinology and Metabolism at Jefferson Medical College and also as a Pfizer fellow in Clinical Pharmacology at St. Vincent's Medical Center. He has written a number of books dealing with medicine, health and social values. His career deals primarily with bringing new therapies to patients with diseases and disabilities. He brought the natural substance, carnitine, into the United States and personally conducted the first clinical study on it. He managed through a fascinating journey to obtain FDA approval for the then fatal disease in children, Primary Carnitine Deficiency, and also for renal dialysis patients. He was the physician responsible for launching lithium for the treatment of bipolar disease.

In 1976 he founded FIM, the Foundation for Innovation in Medicine, whose mission is to accelerate medical discovery, www.fimdefelice.org.

The DeFelice Library

Non-fiction

Drug Discovery: The Pending Crisis, 1972
From Oysters to Insulin: Nature and Medicine at Odds, 1986
Memory Loss: Normal vs. Abnormal, 1988
La Revolution Nutraceutique, 1990
Nutraceuticals: Developing, Claiming and Marketing Medical Foods, 1998
The Carnitine Defense, 1999
The Attack on the White Male – And the Weakening of America, 2010
Maybe-Ism: The Emoji Brain in Search of a Personal God, 2018
Grandpa's Words of Wisdom: Where You Are, Where You're Heading, And What To Do About It, 2021

Fiction

Old Italian Neighborhood Values, 2002
He Made Them Young Again, 2006
Dr. Julian: What Woman Do You Want Me to Be? A Doctor's Gender Sexploration with Three Women, 2017

Biography

A Maverick's Odyssey, One Doctor's Quest to Conquer Disease by Michael Mannion, 2007

Contents

Chapter 1

YOGI BERRA AND YOUR
FORK IN THE ROAD

Dear Olivia and Stephen Carlos,

Though I'm your grandfather who loves you, it breaks my heart to say it but you are historical freaks! The time-honored traditional foundations of our country–such as family, religion and patriotism –are, at breathtaking speed, inexorably fading away. Nature abhors a vacuum so as these human cultural values are leaving us they are being replaced and sucked into the vacuum by other cultural values –and this, largely unbeknown to you and others, is precisely what's happening at this very moment. And it's not, as we shall see, very good news.

I've spent lots of thoughtful on-again, off-again moments trying to decide whether I should write this book, but finally made up my mind to go forward as an obligation to let you know how increasingly the pervasive technology revolution is controlling almost every aspect of your and all other lives. And it is relentless, and unstoppable. The wise, ancient Greek philosopher, Socrates, once said, *"Gnothi seauton"* or "Know thyself." I believe it was another Greek, Menander, who urged us also to know others. Your grandfather adds to their wise advice by urging you to, "Know where the hell you are!" And the only way to accomplish these three is by developing Aristotle's fundamental principle of life, to: "Observe, observe and observe."

1

So you're now probably thinking, "Grandpa, get to the point. What's your book all about?" *It's about all four of the aforementioned, but, unfortunately, I must warn you that it's not about a formula on how to find happiness in these increasingly turbulent times but an attempt to advise you of the dynamics of such change in order to help you adapt to them—if, of course, you want to.* You may simply choose to ignore such dynamics and happily go meekly along with, as water in a stream, the flow of all-controlling technology. It's the choice you will eventually have to make.

And now to Yogi Berra: Yogi was a baseball Hall of Fame catcher for the New York Yankees. Berra was perhaps just as well-known, if not more so, for his demeanor off the field than his play on it. His "nonsensical and sagacious" pronouncements about life, known colloquially as "Yogi-isms," were well known. One famous example was, *"It ain't over till it's over."*

Now, Olivia, you are age 19 and in your first remote Zoom college year, and Stephen Carlos, you are age 16, midway through the high school system. You both are historical freaks in that you currently live on the bridge in the traditional-reality and the new technology driven world and have arrived at the fork in this road. And here's what Yogi had to say about that: *"When you come to a fork in the road, take it."* This was based on the true story of when he gave directions to his friend, Joe Garagiola, when driving to his Montclair home. The town even renamed a local street in his honor: Yogi Berra Way. And yes—the street has a fork in it!

Another famous Montclair resident is the astronaut Buzz Aldrin, who was on the first mission to the moon. My colleague and friend, Patricia Park, was a football game dancer at Montclair High and marched in the town's Buzz Aldrin Day Parade, shaking her pom-poms! Her father coincidentally had a crush on Buzz's younger sister, Madeline, when they were in kindergarten.

In the following pages, I'll cover a broad range of subjects such as the nature of technology, people, government, sex, and religion, in order to help you adapt and take your fork in the road. Because of unstoppable, dominating forces of the technology juggernaut and how it will impact the power structure not only of our country but of the world, I hopefully will convince both of you to try to adapt to it rather than going with the flow and losing your humanity.

And now a few comments before I move on: It's now self-evident that there are many forces in our country whose mission it is to control speech by, in a variety of ways, diminishing the freedom of Americans to express one's opinion. And they're doing a highly effective job at it. Also, there are core human traits that largely prevent men and women from confronting and objectively analyzing the truth. I call this human trait, "the syndrome of the segmental intellect." For example, if I criticize certain aspects of conservatism, conservatives would reflexively assume I'm a liberal and emotionally reject other aspects of my presentation. If I do the same with certain aspects of liberalism, I would be considered a conservative by liberals and the syndrome would naturally follow.

My father or your great grandfather, Stefano, was my only true mentor in my life, and I paid attention to his words of wisdom. He was born in Italy and emigrated to the United States with his family at the age of twelve. Since he had to work to help support his family he never even completed high school. He was a self-educated man, learning to play the violin and other string instruments. He worked his way up to be a captain in the Philadelphia police force and taught law and emergency medicine at the Philadelphia Police Academy. He composed music and even had patents to prevent the impact of torpedoes.

When I was a teenager he told me that people are too busy handling life's daily problems and don't have enough time to think things through. Whatever the reason, it is what it is.

Given the aforementioned and other realities, you can rest assured that your grandfather will call it as he sees it, in order to guide you through this freakish and frightening age of exploding technology.

And finally, never, never and never forget Rudyard Kipling's famous warning, "Make sure you know what size animal you are before you enter the jungle!"

Love,
Grandpa

P.S. You may be wondering why in this book I'm not addressing it to your first cousin, and my grandson, Maximillian Albrecht. This book is meant for high school and early college students before they cross the Rubicon into the world of technology. Max is now almost thirty and has made some solid judgements about life. Later on in the book he will offer some advice to you both, based on his life's experiences.

Chapter 2

THE BIG THREE QUESTIONS: WHAT, WHY AND HOW?

As I said before, spurred on by the Internet, swarms of individuals, groups and institutions are invading and attempting to control your minds regarding your beliefs, both of life in general and life in particular. Learning to employ the Big Four previously mentioned categories will not only help to expose their faults but bring you to a gratifying superior level of intellection and understanding.

This is not an easy discipline to employ but it's absolutely necessary in your journey to adapt to modernism, once more, if you want to. So pay extra and disciplined attention!

I'm not the Facebook type, but due to the insistence and know-how of a friend, I finally joined the team, but only occasionally deal with it. After the last presidential election and the defeat of our controversial president, a Facebook post read, "Finally we can come together and achieve national happiness." Now, though it's psychologically difficult for both of you to do, get together in a room, leave your smart phone in another room, close the door, and together try to analyze this message in depth and *define, with words*, the answers to the following questions.

First of all, ask, "What is happiness?" Then, after your many attempts to define it, choose one and then ask, "Why is that?" After you've agreed on 'that' ask, "What is national happiness?" After you arrive at some definition, then ask, "How do we achieve national happiness?" and after that ask, "Why is it important?"

Now, let me tell you what's going to happen if you are sincere in your efforts and make the commitment to hang in there. Try as you may, if you are intellectually honest, you both will not even be able to specifically answer the first question, let alone the following ones! But choose one anyway and continue to similarly answer the following ones.

By going through this exercise you will enter into a new level of intellectual ability, honesty and humility which will help immensely in adapting to the rapidly escalating modern world challenges.

You will, paradoxically, also become rapidly discouraged for if you attempt to employ this approach to a broad range of subject matter, you'll go crazy. It's best to limit this to critical, selected topics such as freedom, racism, rights, socialism, horse's ass, equality, media, love and marriage, and learn about the overwhelming lack of explaining and understanding them by using words. You must realize that we use words that are extremely limited to explain much in life.

The great intellect and poet, T.S. Elliot, always struggled with finding the right words and wrote, "It's strange that words are so inadequate. Yet, like the asthmatic struggling for breath, so the lover must struggle for words."

You may have the impression that I'm a kind of nihilist, believing that we can really know very little about anything because of the limitation of words. Not so. In the next chapter, I'll discuss how what I call the Emoji brain plays a critical role in both seeking and finding the truth.

Chapter 3

TRUST YOUR EMOJI BRAIN AND NOT WORDY ARGUMENTS

Olivia and Stephen Carlos, this, in a real sense, is one of the most important chapters for you to read and absorb. Paradoxically, it can be one of the most boring, so I'll try to make it easy, but pay extra attention anyway! It deals with the subject of how and what you or I or anyone else can know: what is true, not true, and knowable and not knowable, and how we can make these judgments. The branch of philosophy which deals with this subject is called epistemology. Unfortunately, it is one of the most complicated fields in philosophy with many types of proposed formulas or systems proposing ways on how we know or can know about the myriad faces of reality.

Epistemology is unlike the physical sciences which employ mathematics and the scientific method: 2+2=4 and the speed of light is 186,000 miles per second, and that's that. There's no doubt about it. If, however, a student who majors in philosophy and matriculates for four years at a reputable university, secular or religious, is asked what he or she can know, they will be understandably confused or embrace a woefully faulty system simply because *all systems are faulty!* The deeper one probes, the deeper, as in quicksand, one sinks.

So what's the core problem? It, as I said before, has to do with the use of the inadequacy of words which are, paradoxically, used to define and express things. Now, it's generally agreed that the evolutionary rationale for the development of language was for communication and not to define

7

things. Take a look at the following questions and try to define them or at least adequately describe them with words:

- Is there such a thing as "a" tree?
- What's the difference between a dingbat and horse's ass?

Plato justifiably believed that there are many types of trees and that "the" or pure tree doesn't exist on earth but must exist somewhere. And that is in the World of Ideas somewhere in the universe. His pupil, Aristotle, disagreed and correctly proposed that the "a" tree is in the mind after he had observed many trees over the years with a commonality of traits –trunks, leaves, roots *et al.*

Regarding the difference between a dingbat and a horse's ass, let's suppose that the three of us are having a conversation with a woman on politics. Her opinions are not only way off the wall, but she is arrogant and cocky. We, without saying a word, would exchange glances among the three of us sending the message that the woman is a horse's ass. No words needed! And a few days later we encounter another woman whose political opinions are also way off the wall but delivered with a smiling, warm and sincere demeanor. We would then exchange glances concluding that's she's a dingbat. Once more, not a word spoken.

Now catch this: the lesson of "a" tree and the two women confirms the existence of those three pounds of flesh, the Emoji Brain, which without the use of reason and words, can observe and interpret life's events and experiences.

With each passing day, the brain encounters enormous numbers of human experiences that are not only, but in some mysterious ways are stored, in the brain and become connected and analyzed responding to what the brain perceives. *The Emoji brain then perceives much of the world as Emoji symbols or icons without the use or need of words.* We concluded that there is "a" tree icon by experiencing all kinds of different Emoji trees not by the use of words. Our Emoji brains interpreted and distinguished the difference between a dingbat and horse's ass by past icon experiences and not by the use of words.

Now let's take a look at how the Emoji brain reacts to two types of accidents, one humorous and one of concern, on an ice skating rink. If two teenagers are ice skating together and one falls on her butt, the Emoji event or momentary icon is a cause of laughter even for the young lady sitting on the ice. If, however, a cry of anguish accompanied by the facial body language of suffering is let out by the young lady, then humor takes a back seat and is replaced by concern, the degree of which depends upon the icons of the body image and the sound of the outcry. Getting back to a teenager, if she's skating with her elderly grandmother and the latter falls on the ice, cries or not, it's an instantaneous Emoji icon that causes immediate alarm to the teenager and surrounding witnesses. If, however, your brain identifies a person who falls as a real bad selfish character, this icon may invoke joy internally but feigned concern externally. It's interesting to note that these reactions can take place in less than a spilt second in those three pounds of flesh. How does this happen?

The above was a rather dramatic example of an Emoji symbol or icon, but the millions of them that exist are not. Take taste, for example. One very famous example that you will undoubtedly learn about in your educational journey is that of Marcel Proust and the madeleine, a type of French pastry that he regularly consumed when he was a child. Time passed, and one day, as an adult, after he took a bite of the pastry, it immediately brought back memories of his childhood past.

Regarding smell, many years ago I was a guest in my older brother Larry's home, sleeping in the upstairs bedroom. I was awakened by the smell of pasta sauce or gravy being prepared by my Irish sister-in-law, Pat, using the same recipe of my deceased mother, a mother to be envied! As soon as the odor passed through my nasal cavity and entered my brain's neural circuits, I immediately had an image of my mother in the kitchen stirring the pasta sauce and wearing the green, flowered apron I had made for her when I was in middle school.

Now let's turn to an interesting Emoji event of the combination of sound and smell: it's flatulence or passing gas, otherwise called a fart. If, for example, it occurs at a dinner table with guests, it can be a cause of embarrassment or laughter, depending on the situation, such as whether or not there is an accompanying smell. In any event, it will be a cause of much-needed humor.

One of my favorite quotes regarding the mystery and impact of sound regarding a cause of curiosity was made by Charles Lamb, a famous essayist of the past, who wrote, "Not many sounds in life, and I include all urban and all rural sounds, exceed in interest a knock at the door."

There are untold numbers of body language icons. Bad news. The body slumps. Good news. The eyes light up. Bored or tired. Both yawn-producers. Disbelief. The eyes roll back and the jaw drops.

To me, silence is not the absence of sound, but one of the most essential, message-producing Emoji icons. It leads you to thoughtful analysis of the many avenues of life, including communicating with oneself. It can take you to higher spiritual levels coming up with creative ideas and solutions. Silence is a critical key in adapting to the technological revolution and will be discussed later on.

Before we go on, I didn't get into the numerous philosophic epistemological systems simply because they are too numerous, and, to boot, there is no agreement among philosophers regarding which is the correct one you should appreciate when you are exposed to your instructors who teach the stuff using inadequate words. I'm not being cynical about this for it's just the way it is. The following are two examples which will give you a feel of what you'll face out there in our educational system:

Let's start with the incomparable Aristotle, the most synthetic mind ever to exist. He is not only called "the Philosopher" of all philosophers but also the father of logic, biology and meteorology, and a few other categories. Oftentimes, when I'm feeling that I'm a pretty bright guy, I think of Aristotle and then immediately eat humble pie. He created the syllogism as a critical tool in the use of reason. An example is as follows:

Humans are rational

Herman is a human

Therefore Herman is rational

Make sense to you? It does to me, but not to many philosophers, because the primary assumption, that only humans are rational is not universally true. For example, chimpanzees can behave rationally, so Herman can be a chimpanzee. Don't laugh, for this type of reasoning is serious stuff in philosophic circles.

Deconstructionism is a natural extension of what is known as analytic philosophy, whose major advocate was the extremely brilliant Jacques Derrida, who was obsessed with the meaning of words. Poor guy! An example to where his intensive search for meaning of word-based language was given to me by a friend. Just as someone was about to enter a hotel elevator, he noticed a poster on the side saying, "Only seeing-eye dogs permitted." A deconstructionist would interpret it as a warning that humans aren't permitted to enter the elevator, let alone with their baggage as well as with regular dogs or anyone or anything else. Imagine employing this type of reasoning in every aspect of life where words are used, the meaning of which are not precise and elaborate which can be interpreted in multiple ways. It would drive one to insanity before the first sunset. I sometimes wonder how Derrida handled his intense search for the meaning of words without going out of his mind.

I hope you guys weren't bored by this epistemological journey, but make sure you understand this dilemma before you move on in the book.

Chapter 4

THE DARK SIDE OF TECHNOLOGY

I don't need to tell you about the vast and growing world of technology spurred on by Google, Twitter, Facebook, the virtual world of devices, robots–you name it. Now you know that your grandfather is a technological dinosaur and somewhat of a hermit. As one ages some become less tolerant of people. I do not text or use GPS. I did learn to text way back and did it only once because I immediately received three replies from that single text and feared the message invasion of the future if I were to expand my contacts. I also observed others whose world was invaded by texting with their necks bent and thumbs in constant motion isolated from observing and learning about the real world that surrounds them.

During the Covid invasion, many men and women took strolls passing by my home, oftentimes when I was busy landscaping my property. One day, a couple passed by pushing a baby carriage. The man had his right hand on the carriage bar and the lady her left one. Both with their free hands were on their cellphones, angrily screaming aloud in their own worlds while the baby was also screaming. I was maybe five yards away and neither recognized my existence and my body language of obvious displeasure. A few minutes, later a pretty little girl about 7 years-old rode by on her bicycle, talking to her cellphone which was perched on the middle of her handlebars in front of her face. As a car was approaching she, in her non-observing world, steered to the left in front of it. Luckily, the alert driver swerved to the right and jammed on his brakes just in the nick of time. I angrily reprimanded her and ordered her to remove the phone, to no avail. She, instead, ignored me and sped off speaking to her gadget. This event, apart from the danger to the girl, mightily disturbed me, for it sent an unsettling message about how parents are losing control over their children because of the growing pervasive and tenacious tentacles of technology.

There's another technology which, like the consumption of marijuana, is exploding. They are gadgets such as Fitbit wristbands which, 24/7, are warning and measuring many biological parameters such as one's cardiovascular status, and potential sleep apnea. In my limited experience with approximately a dozen wearers, they are addicted to this technology, frequently checking the recordings, even while having dinner.

There's another gadget that's attached to the body which constantly measures blood sugar, eliminating the need of the usual painful pricking of the finger with a needle. Now there are approximately 34 million diabetics in the United States, and do not be surprised if a majority of them will heartedly embrace this gadget constantly checking their blood sugars every hour, creating millions of gadget-dependent, overly concerned patients. As an endocrinologist who, in my early career, specialized in diabetes, I can say this is not at all necessary to adequately control their diabetes for a substantial majority of them.

And, don't be surprised if a large percentage of diabetics also wear their Fitbit or other gadgets addicted to measuring the oncoming numerous parameters.

My grandchildren, don't ever fall in love with such creatures!

Regarding robots, an old-timer friend of mine told me that he cannot live without being with and conversing with his Alexa. A Japanese colleague told me that his friend purchased a life-size speaking female robot where she—or he?—is programed to say what he wants to hear. He fell in love with and subsequently actually married her. Similar robots are becoming more commonplace in our country.

A few years ago, I gave a lecture to a large group at a retirement community, after which I asked the members what they thought about their lives in their new-found home. A number of them said that they previously were bored-stiff and couldn't wait to enter the virtual world of goggles or some other device where they could choose their own world of pleasure and adventure in order to cast away their boredom. Boredom is a much more painful condition than many of our physical diseases.

Now here's an experience that is both amusing and scary which deals with GPS. I had my office in Manhattan about 30 miles from home, for nearly half a century, commuted every weekday and could drive there with my eyes closed, even at my current age. At home, I occasionally have appointments at locations about a couple miles away, and I sometimes need directions on how to get there. Since I don't use GPS, I frequently call, asking directions to these locations. And the following is usually what happens:

"Can you give me directions on how to get to your office?"

(Pause; and then)

"Do you do GPS?"

"No."

"Please wait a second, and I'll talk to someone here who may know."

(Pause; about 30 seconds)

"Sorry sir; there's no one in the office who knows the directions."

"But can someone at least give the general directions? You know, the major streets, where I can at least have an idea where you're located?"

(Pause; about 15 seconds)

"I'm sorry sir; no one in the office seems to know."

These repetitive encounters got me thinking about what would happen if a hostile country would explode a single nuclear weapon in outer space that would shut down our satellite GPS almost everywhere? How would people know how to arrive to their desired destinations for help, or to help their loved ones and others? How would it impact our military capability?

And, by the way, such a bomb would shut down much of our national electrical grid system creating other enormous problems, one practical one being during the cold winter season where home heating is electricity dependent.

Multi-millions would be technology deprived, leading to a national paralysis and, as with sudden narcotic addiction withdrawal, a massive psychological breakdown and paralysis of will.

Olivia and Stephen Carlos, just think about the ramifications of the aforementioned catastrophic possibilities and the many more that are on their way. (It's a type of natural obsessional behavior.)

What is your honest, well-thought-out opinion regarding the following? Technology is increasingly taking over and controlling much of our personal and non-personal behavior, from the Internet to personal robots which is rapidly robbing you of your privacy. There is an exploding feeding frenzy that is growing way out of control. Every time you turn to or employ technology someone knows about it and can use it for good, evil or simple curiosity. Bottom line, because of this, someone or some institution has the capacity to increasingly control your mind and body somehow, someway.

I read the following which should scare the daylights out of you:

"Google dominates all search engines controlling 91.54 percent of the market. The next closest is Bing at 2.44 percent. Google handles an estimated 2 trillion searches per year worldwide, 167 billion per month, 5.5 billion searches per day, 228 million searches per hour, 3.8 million searches per minute, and 63,000 searches per second. In the time it will take you to read this sentence, Google will field hundreds of thousands of searches."

Now, my grandchildren, did you ever wonder who at Google has access to such information and how these men and women, in a number of ways, can use it to further their objectives, even personal ones? Hopefully, you don't have any enemies working there or at any other Big Tech corporations.

And here's an example where I'd like you to employ the "why" exercise. Both of you, as well as a significant number of technology users, know that one surrenders their privacy and independence to others when in cyberspace. Your life is being increasingly controlled and, as I said, almost entirely supervised–even by simply carrying your smartphone so that your parents or an unknown third party can locate and contact you and even know your whereabouts. Your out-of-home lives are almost completely supervised by adults, be it at soccer or sleepovers. You can take supervised karate classes but you are punished if you even push someone in the schoolyard who had insulted your mother.

One crucial message and that which most concerns me, is that being immersed in the technology tsunami robs you of the time to think and adapt to what it's doing to you in order to accommodate to life's increasing complexities.

Now let me tell you something about my life. I was born on April 14th, the day Lincoln was assassinated and the Titanic sank. During the period spanning from my 1936 birth to 2021, I observed and experienced the most radical exploding, unsettling and destabilizing change in human history fueled by highly intrusive technology. Folks my age are the true historians of this era. Future ones will have to depend on what has been recorded.

Now put yourselves in my place. I, a first-generation Italian, was born in Philadelphia in a small row house in an old Italian neighborhood housing many hardworking Italian immigrants. There were no telephones or television. We did, however, have a radio, in our home. Every weeknight, with eager anticipation and lying on the floor, I listened to a number of adventure episodes, my favorite being the Lone Ranger, which was accompanied by Rossini's energetic William Tell Overture score. When I was about nine, the beginning of the technology explosion in our home arrived when a television and telephone entered our home. There were only three television channels, and the phone was a party-line one shared by two or more homes.

At about age fourteen, I decided to go to work and started as a shoeshine boy. I carefully chose my street corner near a pool room where the younger Italians with money congregated. I worked Friday and Saturday afternoons and nights. At night, I went to two local bars where the guys were feeling good and generous, drinking mostly beer, and where they were much bigger tippers than the afternoon guys. I gave my earnings to my mother, who put most of it away as savings. I never took an allowance in my working years which meant almost most of the time. A couple of years later, I set up a hot dog and soda stand outside Shibe Park ballpark, later known as Connie Mack Stadium, that housed the baseball teams, the Philadelphia Phillies, the Philadelphia Athletics and the football team, the Philadelphia Eagles. As time passed, and as a teenager, I had other jobs such as parking cars and working in a gas station. During my college days, I was a supervisor of a city playground where those youngsters taught me how to play chess, but where I never won a game. Go figure! During medical school, I had an eye-opening learning experience in charge, by myself, in what we used to call an accident ward which is now called an emergency room, and what an experience it was! More about this later on.

So, you may be wondering what's my point? Well, there are two essential, life-teaching ones, but before we get to them, let's get back to me.

Around the age of 12, something happened that profoundly changed my life. My father and mentor began to teach me about philosophy. I read and thought about the ideas of many of them, but it was that great giant, incomparable intellect, Aristotle, who sent me on a disciplined path that changed my life. Among his pearls of wisdom, there were, to repeat, those three words that struck me like a lightning bolt regarding how to handle life. They were "Observe, observe, observe." And it became almost a constant habit and part of my persona which ability to observe and learn increased with increased usage over time.

You probably know about the great Renaissance genius and artist, Leonardo Da Vinci. One of his favorite themes to young artists was *saper vedere,* or knowing how to see, when walking through the fields observing various objects. He wrote, "As you go through the fields, turn your attention to various objects, and in turn now at this thing and now at that, collecting a store of diverse facts … Do not do as some painters do who… though they see the objects, do not comprehend them."

Now, Olivia and Stephen Carlos, here's what I would strongly urge you to do, but don't tell your mother and father, whatever you do–play hooky from school once in a while! *An Apology for Idlers* is one of my favorite teaching short stories written by Robert Louis Stevenson, the author of *Dr. Jekyll and Mr. Hyde.* It's about a boy caught playing hooky from school by an elderly man who scolds him for missing important educational lessons in the classroom. But his arguments were no match for the wisdom of this young lad. He, with razor-sharp reasoning, defends the critical importance of being both idle and alone in silence, because it released his brain's curiosity to observe, wonder and think about life on his own in order to adapt to real life instead of from what's being fed to him in a classroom. It's a must-read for both of you and, hopefully, will persuade you to develop the discipline to be periodically totally alone with yourselves observing, observing and observing.

And now, on to the nature of mankind. It's people!

Chapter 5

WHAT PEOPLE ARE REALLY LIKE

My grandchildren, I've been heavily criticized when I tell folks about my attempt to tell you the unvarnished truth about people, organizations, government and patterns of life. The reason? The truth is not pleasant and oftentimes brutal, and you guys are too young and not experienced enough to handle this reality. They say, with some justification, that for a number of reasons you are, believe it or not, currently in the happiest period of your lives and why prematurely ruin it? After all, there's plenty of time to learn about life and experience as time unfolds, and there's no need to hurry.

I listened carefully and, frankly speaking, was tempted to lay down my pen but then concluded that because of the accelerating pace of technology there will not be sufficient time for you to normally mature, and the time, therefore, is now.

So here goes!

Life is a relentless battle between evil and good in all cultures in all times perpetrated by people where the net effect of evil is, unfortunately, the clear winner. Or, as some people believe, there is no such thing as evil and good, and as Shakespeare wrote, "There is nothing either good or bad but thinking makes it so." Don't believe it! Just use your Emoji brain and take a look at an icon video on concentration camps during wars.

Let's take a look at some words that either directly or indirectly reflect what many cultures may consider evil. But also, let's not forget that such words are interpreted as Emoji icons or symbols being difficult to precisely define with words themselves. For example, on the evil list is pornography.

In a case on pornography brought before the Supreme Court and in an attempt to define it, Justice Potter said something like, "Though you can't define pornography, you know it when you see it." Also, there are words that, depending how you use them, can have a dual meaning. For example, *selfishness,* where Jesus said in the Golden Rule, "Do unto others as you would do unto yourself." In other words, it's okay to be selfish. Also, *patriotism* used to be considered unequivocally good but now is at the fork in the road on its way to becoming considered evil in our country.

The following are some examples of words considered as evil, but it's important to know that, to repeat, sometimes they can have dual meanings: hate, cruelty, envy, murder, jealousy, sex (many types ranging from pedophilia to adultery), treachery, selfishness, traitor, disrespect, cruelty, cowards, mendacity, blasphemy, torture, deceitfulness, avarice, gluttony, sins of many other types depending on the culture and, the Big Kahuna, physical and mental disease.

In the Bible evil is mentioned throughout its pages, such as in the Ten Commandments. In Christian teachings there are the Seven Deadly Sins and in Dante's Inferno there's lust, greed, sloth, wrath, envy and pride.

Speaking of words with double meeting, Dante considered pride one of the worse sins, but today it has a mixed connotation depending on how it's used. It's interesting to note that Aristotle pointed out that the Greek language lacked a word for well-earned pride.

The following are examples of words considered as good: love, family, charity, friends, courage, prayer, patience, kindness, happiness and altruism.

Bottom line, life is tough and not a bowl of cherries and the battle between the evil and the good life is universally considered Manichean. Mani was a 3ʳᵈ century heretic Christian prophet who preached that the world is a battle between good and evil or light and dark forces and humans are the players in which this battle is fought.

Regarding experiencing happiness in this life which, in major part is the net result between the battle of good and evil, it's impressively described by the cynical humorist, W.C. Fields, when he advised, "Smile first thing in the morning. Get it over with!"

THE BIG SIX HUMAN CHARACTERISTICS

Before I go on to discuss life's two major forces that determine our destiny, *suffering and searching*, let's take a look at some big picture core principles of human behavior. Many great minds have formulated other principles but these are the ones that I prefer in order to get right to the point. The Big Six are extremely helpful to more easily understand your own as well as the behavior of other folks be they here in our country or in a remote Manchurian community. To be sure, this exercise might not be very pleasant, but it will no doubt be enlightening.

- *Self-interest:* Self-interest is self-evident. It's operational from the cradle to your last waking moment. Men and women wake up each morning thinking about themselves from what to wear, how they look and how to get through the day. You, as students, study in order to achieve a passing grade or even earn honors. Stephen Carlos, after school, you play all kinds of video games with competitors, even in faraway countries. Olivia, you frequently enter cyberspace in order to converse with other friends on a *quid pro quo* social basis. In other words, I'll listen to you if you listen to me. Self-interest drives all forms of human behavior. After all, we all welcome the opportunity to speak to others about what's on our minds. And lastly, self-interest and one's security are inextricably intertwined.

- *Self-deception or Rationalization:* These are, in a sense, very similar human dynamics so I listed them together under a single category. This is a huge characteristic that all people, and I mean all, do not recognize among themselves let alone how others employ it. This means that humans deceive themselves almost daily to maintain a belief or position that is not true or that they have not sufficiently thought through in order to be comfortable or protect their egos from being proven incorrect.

  Olivia, you are a confident and intelligent young woman with admirable social skills. Do you remember when I tested you on your self-deception nature? When I learned that you had an interest in becoming a medical doctor, I told you that female doctors are not as good as male ones. Well, your face turned red, and you huffed and puffed and passionately denied it. But you hadn't the slightest idea of learning what was behind my reasoning committing a classic act of self-deception. Your heated reaction also involved the characteristic of stubbornness. Don't forget there's a difference between stubbornness and being strong-willed. The former is a recalcitrant position one takes out of pride without trying to analyze the facts and the latter occurs after such open objective analysis after which you should stand your ground.

Stephen Carlos, you, at your age are developing superb analytic talents and have selected Conservatism over Progressive Liberalism as your political philosophy of choice. When, however, I mentioned that President Biden, who represents the latter political philosophy, has some reasonable ideas, your analytic mind turned off and, like your sister, was not inclined to hear and digest the reasoning behind my argument. But I must say, forgive me Olivia, that I believe your sister is a bit more inflexible than you.

Rationalization is a subdivision of self-deception where one uses faulty reasoning in order to convince oneself and others of the rightness of their position. Sounds familiar? The great Aristotle defined "man as a rational creature." Your grandfather defines "man as a creature who rationalizes."

- *Recognition:* You can see this personal trait from childhood, where children begin to show off to their parents, relatives and others, to entertainers and politicians and everyone in between. There's an innate mental pleasure to be recognized and many people will go to great costs to be recognized on the various platforms of life, such as Facebook or Instagram.
- *Power-Money:* These are, in a certain sense, the same thing. Money buys power and power gets money. They are operational in all walks of life and more operational than ever before. They are thrilling to possess and, as with recognition, people will oftentimes go to cruel extremes to possess them.
- *Competition:* It's found in the same places as self-interest, power, money and recognition. For example, one commonly competes in order to achieve power, money and recognition because of

21

self-interest. It's a driving force from kindergarten to the presidency of the United States. And, in large part, competition is based on the existence of both followers and their leaders which we'll examine later on.

- *Altruism:* For me, this is the most powerful, universal and innate human characteristic that offers a glimmer of hope for the future of mankind. Altruism is a term that was coined by the French philosopher, Auguste Comte, during the nineteenth century. It's a derivation of the Italian word, *altrui*, which means "to others." I would define it as *an innate, universal frame of mind which makes people want or feel the need to help others and at times leads to action to do so.* A classic example was recently reported about a man during the 2020 Christmas season who, with a thousand dollars in cash, was about to enter a store to purchase a smartphone when he observed someone nearby from the Salvation Army in freezing weather asking for donations for the poor. The man then hesitated, gave it some thought and decided to donate the money to the Salvation Army and deprive himself of his much-desired phone. He didn't give his name and no one could locate him to give thanks.

  If you think about it, it's the force behind all of the aforementioned "good" word. In a real sense altruism is similar to the Golden Rule which includes the concept of love.

SUFFERING

And now, my dear grandchildren, here's some more news to alert you to what's increasingly coming your way. You will, along with the rest of humanity, suffer mental and physical pain for your entire lives with, thank God, intermittent periods of welcomed relief and fleeting happiness. The great philosopher, Heidegger, believed that just by the act of existing, all of us have what he called, Existential Anxiety. But I would go a step beyond and propose Existential Suffering, which also is that, just by the act of existing, we all suffer for a multiplicity of reasons.

I want both of you to step out of your door and take a stroll around your neighborhood passing about a hundred homes. Within those homes there will be children and adults stricken either with autism, ADHD, depression, anxiety, schizophrenia, cancer, heart disease, arthritis, dementia, loneliness and unhappiness, and a number of other diseases, disabilities and mental states, all of which cause suffering. Also, you are probably not aware of the extent of such maladies that exist in your current family, including your grandfather's!

You may be interested in the time when I first really felt the power and extent of suffering and learned to hate disease. Strangely enough, the only person whom I met in my extensive career in medical research who ever claimed to hate disease was Dr. Druckenmiller, a horse and buggy country doctor in the town where Grandma DeFelice lived before she made the mistake of marrying me. He was a creature of the past when, as a medical student, I went with him on house calls. Many of his patients didn't have much money but instead used barter, a common practice of *quid pro quo*. For example, the families would give him a roasted chicken or pot-roast instead of cash which they didn't have. Boy, did I learn a lot about bedside manners which is almost a forgotten art in today's medical practice being supplanted by cold, economically based medical technology.

One day, right around my puberty time, I noticed my grandmother, who was severely diabetic, was rapidly becoming short of breath. Gradually, she became so weak that she couldn't walk anymore and quickly fell into a deep diabetic coma. In those days, seriously afflicted family members were generally cared for at home for fear of entering a hospital and never leaving which, by the way, had some basis in reality. My family placed my *nonna*, or grandmother, on a bed in our small living room where the members of the family and others could watch over her. We all lived close to one another in the old Italian neighborhood no more than a fifteen-minute walk. Think about that.

There was a continuous 24-hour vigil over *nonna* with my parents, very caring aunts, uncles, cousins and sometimes even neighbors taking turns in about four-hour shifts. The kitchen was alive with family and friends drinking coffee, eating coffee cakes, cinnamon buns and tea biscuits. There was no liquor not only because it was rarely consumed in Italian families but also because it was too expensive. My grandfather, Loreto, or *nonno,* was the exception. He loved his home-made wine in happy times, in sad times and in in-between times. In other words, every day!

Now, Olivia and Stephen Carlos, can you imagine that happening today. You, as with many others, have no neighborhood family. Today, family members are in different states in different countries and communicate by texting or Zoom. You rarely touch them—no handshake, no hug, no kiss, no nothing—a crucial factor in all types of essential human communication.

One night I found myself alone with my *nonna* while her coma deepened. I remember like it was yesterday placing my face nose-to-nose next to hers and talking to her. I said, "Look, *Nonna*, if you can hear me, smile, or say or do something. Give me a sign." But nothing happened. I just stared at her in the palpable stillness and silence. It bothered me that even I could not get a response from her, such was my juvenile confidence. Then came the Big Bang. I felt a powerful feeling that would consume me for the rest of my medical career. There were two elements to this feeling. The first was an intense hatred of disease and the second, a strong conviction that disease must be conquered.

I remember thinking that if I could just place my finger though her skull and move her brain in the right direction, she would come out of her coma. That was my first attempt as a doctor diagnostician. I don't know by what logic I came to this conclusion, but I decided that I did not have the ability to move anything in her brain by myself so I logically asked myself who could? Where could I go for help? I decided to go to the local Catholic Church and talk to God, one-on-one.

In those days the church doors were always open and not locked up at night as they are today, which I understand because of today's unsettling culture. It was about midnight when I entered the church. I knelt before the crucifix and began to bargain with God promising that I would do this and that if he would allow my *nonna* to live. This type of bargaining, as I said before, is called a *quid pro quo* "foxhole prayer": the kind of prayer that soldiers make in the heat of battle by imploring, "Lord, if you allow me to survive this life-threatening danger, I promise to repent and go to church every week." I often wonder how many times these promises are kept.

On my way home, I was quite confident that I had made a deal with God. It was around one in the morning when I got home, and my parents were steaming mad and worried why I hadn't told them that I would be going to the church. Our small home was surprisingly crowded at that hour with relatives and friends eating pastries and, paradoxically, filled with laughter which at first bothered me, but afterwards, I appreciated its cathartic value as a way to lighten the pain of certain sad and even tragic moments.

In any event, my mother ordered me to bed. Because I was confident that my deal with God was sealed, I was relaxed and fell asleep as soon as my head hit the pillow. But when I woke up late the next morning, I saw that my *nonna* was not on the living room bed. She had died and her body had been taken to a funeral home. Needless to say, I had a bone to pick with the Boss!

It was about 15 years later when I was a medical student covering the pediatric ward, which brought back memories of my *nonna* that night. I was caring for a frail nine-year old child with terminal leukemia. She was bloated with steroids and hemorrhaging into her skin and internal organs. Her mother and father knelt by her bedside silently praying while others stood by also in heavy silence. The scene of Christ and the manger came to mind, the big difference being that one dealt with the giving of life and the other with its taking. I, and the two wonderful nurses, felt the extraordinary metaphysical power of this silence.

I left to take care of other children, and when I returned and examined her I discovered she was gone—forever. I had to tell the parents. I tried my mightiest not to cry and somehow succeeded. I also tried to persuade the nurses, and they were superb and experienced ones, to break the news, but they convinced me that it was my duty as the child's physician and I had to learn to perform such a duty in the future. And so I did.

After the parents and the others left, I was alone with the deceased child and thought that there she is, alive one second and gone the next. As some doctors do at moments such as these, I thought about religious issues and the incomprehensibility of the cruel death of a child. And then, and God knows where this came from in my brain, I suddenly had images of my *nonna* in a coma and her family surrounding her. And I felt what I felt as a young boy: hatred of disease and the need to conquer the beast which, as you will see, fueled my career in medical research.

25

One final note on suffering: during my early teens I remember standing next to the casket of my Aunt Tillie at her wake, a big-hearted and generous woman if there ever was one, when, for some unexplainable reason, the thought occurred to me that moments of suffering in life last much, much longer than moments of joy. Men and women experience and also dwell more on their downer than their upper moments. Thus it's the rare person who oftentimes relates to others how he's feeling great rather than about his problems ranging from his back pain to unhappy family events and their selfish members. Moments of depressed moods generally far outlast the ephemeral, upper ones of joy for unknown and puzzling reasons.

Here's one observation that dawned on me when I was a student in college and resonates even more today. The clear majority of movie films and newsprint, in one way or another, dealt with mental and physical tragedy ranging from downer moments to cruelty to death. These days, with hundreds of television channels instantaneously available with a simple click, I periodically scan scores of them as a learning exercise to determine what attracts people in today's world. Not surprisingly, nothing has changed. It's mostly about unpleasant to tragic subject matter. Even local and national television news channels report mostly downer news from local disputes to potential terrorist attacks. Even cowboy movies with their goodie and baddie characters predominantly deal with killings and betrayals before the very brief segments of happy endings—and they are always brief! I want you to think about why this is so.

What particularly struck me back then and strikes me more so today is the striking lack not only in numbers but in the quality of good comedy. Back in the '80s, I mentioned this to my father during cocktail time. He had also made this observation and concluded that good comedy was much more difficult to compose than shows that deal with betrayal, sickness and horror confirming my previous observation. Our conversation got me thinking again, and here's what I concluded and continue to believe: though on the surface the majority of men and women would strenuously object, the human mind is geared toward dwelling and feeling comfortable dealing with and talking about their suffering.

As a physician, I am well aware and fully appreciate that patients must explain what's ailing them. After all, I'm a patient, and I'm not talking about this scenario. I'm speaking about when such discussions go way beyond that which is understandably warranted but, on the other hand, is quite "natural", which brings me to my theory. It has to do with the evolution of *Homo sapiens* when people confronted ferocious animals, disease without medicines, and tribal wars and the wounding and killing of each other, all suffering situations. So the human brain built in this acceptance of suffering as a human condition and naturally accommodates it, oftentimes to excess. In fact, some keen minds have postulated that people in many ways love to suffer, which I tend to agree with. (There is an Italian proverb – *non perdere buona miseria* – don't waste good agony!)

I just realized that I've made a huge omission that, as we shall see, much good comes from suffering!

But here's a true story that's both a gruesome and beautiful act of heroism. During my long career, I met many leaders both here and abroad of industry, academe, government and medicine, among others. One afternoon a while back I had an unforgettable lunch at the now departed Lespinasse restaurant at the St. Regis Hotel in Manhattan with the chief legal counsel of one of Italy's largest corporations. We were discussing the possibility of another war in Eastern Europe when he, with a sudden burst of emotion, changed the topic and told this story.

During World War II, when he was a teenager, the Germans had occupied Italy. There was a group called the Italian Resistance whose mission was to impede German operations like sabotaging physical structures such as bridges and also to deliver information to the American military regarding the whereabouts of German troops. He bravely volunteered to be a spy for the Resistance. The latter used the small town's Catholic Church in the village to transmit messages back and forth. My friend, while on his bicycle, used to pick up the messages, transmitting them back and forth from the church to the Italian fighters by carrying them tightly tucked in his belt behind his back. One day a German soldier frisked him and, by an act of God, said my friend, he missed the package.

Tragically, when the Germans, for example, suspected that the Resistance was responsible for blowing up a bridge right under their noses, they would punish the men, and not the women, in the local village. My friend then told me a story which made me completely lose my appetite. One day, the Germans correctly identified a man involved in the Resistance who knew where the Resistance soldiers were. They, as one of their various torture techniques, tied him to a stake set up in the village's piazza, and forced all of the townspeople to witness the event. A hot poker was then placed before one eye, and he was told that if he didn't spill the beans and let them know where the Resistance fighters were, they would insert the poker in his eye not only blinding but possibly even killing him. This courageous man refused to squeal. The Germans kept their promise and not only blinded the other eye but cut off part of his tongue to boot. Now the tongue is a very vascular organ so he was bleeding profusely. The women then took the lead and placed and pressured clean rags on his tongue for a long time until the bleeding stopped. The townspeople then took care of the man for the rest of his life.

After finishing his story, tears filled this strong man's eyes and, in a kind of forceful, pleading tone, he exclaimed, "Stefano, no more wars. No more wars." (FYI, Stefano is my first name in Italian.)

You may find this story kind of macabre but it's nothing compared to other cruelties of war. The message is that good or unparalleled heroism can come from evil such as torture.

As we were on our way out he grabbed my arm and in cynical tones he said, "Stefano, I forgot to tell you. The Germans loved their wine and they spared torturing the male winemakers."

"Self-interest," I said to myself.

After our lunch, I wondered how I would do with the menacing poker facing my eyes and concluded that I'm probably not a hero. On the other hand, heroism is something that's not predictable. There are untold numbers of acts of heroism during wartime by men who would not be deemed the heroic type. You only know how you will act if you are there. I faced death three times in my life without experiencing fear. But they were all acute situations where I didn't have much time to think, but only to react. If that hot poker were in front of my eyes lingering for a minute or two, fear would rule the moment and who knows what would transpire.

Now I'm going to tell you a story about the eyes I'll never forget but, because of the importance of confidentiality, personal details will be omitted. When I had my own clinical research organization, I was approached by an international company who had discovered a nerve growth factor in laboratory studies and requested that I put together a plan about how to evaluate its promise in clinical studies. This substance really aroused my interest for, if it were active in humans, it could be used to treat multiple nervous system diseases and trauma from degenerative brain diseases to strokes. I agreed to take the project and assembled, as per my unbudgeable standard procedure, a group of our leading medical experts which I called a Peer Group to help select which medical conditions would be most likely to respond to this promising substance and help design the clinical study in order to properly evaluate the effectiveness and safety of the substance.

Shortly after the initial clinical trials began, I received a phone call from a famous Nobel Prize laureate requesting a private meeting with me, which of course I agreed to even though I hadn't the slightest idea what was the reason behind the request. He was a tall, white-haired and well-dressed man with a distinguished demeanor. At our meeting he asked if I would release to him all the pertinent information on this promising substance for him to review which I readily agreed to do. Interestingly enough, he didn't offer the reason behind his request and, as a courtesy, I didn't ask. When was the last time you heard or read about the word "courtesy?" Think about it.

After his review he requested a meeting with me during which he revealed the nature of his fatal disease which had no known treatment, not even to prolong his life a little. We then thoroughly reviewed the information searching for pieces of it that would theoretically offer hope for the treatment of his malady. Then he abruptly stood up—I then noticed his problem with balance—and passionately asked about my opinion on the probability of success. I reluctantly responded honestly and directly. The substance was not specifically developed for the treatment of his disease. There were no good animal models in which one could test its potential for his condition. Based on my objective medical review, I told him that the probability of success was not good. He then asked me what I would do if I were in his shoes. Based on the absence of any therapies and his certain rendezvous with death, I said I wouldn't hesitate to take the chance. "A kind of Pascal's Wager," he whispered. He paused, graciously thanked me and left with stooped shoulders that were not due to the disease but to crippling despair.

Though we had not planned any clinical trials for his disease, I was moved enough by this encounter and called the president of the company requesting a grant to sponsor such a study. He readily agreed. Frankly speaking, I was pretty happy with myself and immediately visited this good man to tell him the good news and that he could volunteer for the clinical study once I got it going. He said, "Dr. DeFelice, would you give me some time to think about it?" In order to persuade him to make a decision, I gave him two weeks to decide.

Just before the two-week deadline he came to my office, and I noticed that his balance might have slightly worsened, which was not a welcome medical sign. I would rate our meeting as one of the most (tough to come up with the word or words) unforgettable in my long career. It dealt with his eyes. After the initial greeting, hardly a word was spoken. We sat face-to-face in total silence while his eerily, piercing eyes spoke to me with the following words and phrases with shifting messages, "Dr. DeFelice, it's decision-making time. I'm hopeful. I'm not hopeful. I want you to make the decision. Would you convince me? It's really my decision to make. I'm kidding myself, for I know it won't work. Maybe it will work. How could my life end this tragic way with continuing paralysis and eventually becoming a vegetable? Why me? I'll have to give it a little more thought or maybe not. Maybe it's best to quit and surrender to inevitable death."

These were not messages of weakness but a courageous determination to get it over with, one way or another. He once more asked me what I would do, and I told him I would take the substance, for I'd have no other option. Also, if he didn't improve after three months or his clinical status would decline, then that was the appropriate time to make a final decision. He hesitated, paused, stood up, shook my hand, graciously thanked me and left without commenting on my suggestion.

Now, Olivia and Stephen Carlos, this is a superb example of profound silent suffering messaging mixed with a modicum of futile hope detected by my Emoji brain. No words needed! The larger message? Much mental and physical suffering is experienced silently and undetected by others.

I was waiting to hear from him, but after a few weeks I read that this great man had passed away. It is believed that he ended his life rather than face the inexorable downhill path of suffering where he would end up as a vegetable. Needless to say, I thought my advice was the way to go, and he should have waited. But, however, the clinical study results weren't encouraging, so that would have delayed his decision by only a few months while suffering mightily during this period.

And let's not forget there are, thank God, many personal positive results due to suffering. For example, a lady friend of mine was diagnosed with a type of incurable breast cancer. By some unexpected result of standard anti-cancer therapy, she became, to the surprise and delight of her doctors, cured. After her recovery she formed an organization that raised money to contribute to cancer research organizations dedicated to curing this type of cancer.

Stephen Carlos, here's a story for you. During World War II, the Japanese captured about 2,000 U.S. troops in the Philippines and placed them in a camp within their occupied territory and treated them cruelly. You wouldn't believe how cruel! The U.S. military got wind of this, but only after 1,500 of our men had died from malaria, dysentery and starvation. The American commander asked for troop volunteers to sneak behind enemy lines to rescue the 500 remaining troops. There was no need to wait, for a group of military rangers immediately volunteered to risk their lives to save their buddies' lives. They entered Japanese territory needing to hide themselves in the jungle thicket in order to avoid discovery by the surrounding Japanese troops. With the help of Philippine guerillas, they succeeded in overwhelming the Japanese defenders and freed the men, many of whom were extremely weak and on the verge of dying. Despite the odds, the rangers managed to successfully guide the prisoners though thirty miles of jungle back to safety. In traditional language, these rangers would be considered heroes, let alone real men.

Now compare these rangers to college male students who, with encouragement from their professors, run to safe places within university walls in order to avoid having hurt feelings triggered by a speaker whose opinions emotionally disturb them. I have mixed feelings about these males because they are the product of the system which encourages them to do so. Unfortunately for them, despite the blessings of the universities, I don't think the general student body would consider them real men, but maybe not.

Over the years, I've come across a number of parents who sacrificed the pleasures of life such as a vacation and dining out once in a while, to save enough money to send their children to college. Here's a fact that's rarely mentioned today. I've travelled to many countries in my career, and there is none like the United States where charity abounds. Now why do you think this secret is kept? Think about it.

You are still too young to be aware of, let alone appreciate, that millions of such acts of suffering result into beautiful positive outcomes from the small to the large. One principal reason that you, as well as others, don't hear about them because they, as I've mentioned before, are not newsworthy.

SEARCHING

Because of, or maybe in spite of suffering during one's entire existence, the mind is understandably programmed to continually search for ways to alleviate or get rid of the mental and physical conditions of pain beyond just the availability of food and shelter. It's part of the genetic evolutionary disposition of mankind. Thus, way back in the earliest cultures the search for medicines or other remedies is evident. Over 8,000 years ago in the pre-Incas culture, people chewed on the cocaine-containing coca leaf to reduce fatigue and the stress of life as well as alleviate depression, an increasingly common condition today. Over 3,000 years ago in parts of the Middle East, opium was taken for pain, to induce sleep and for its pleasurable, soporific mental effects.

But what is both puzzling and fascinating is the existence of another type of universal search over and above the aforementioned. It's what I call the Transcendental Search which is a search for the meaning or purpose of life beyond that of life's daily routine such as the existence of a universal force or the nature of an after-life where we may meet and rejoice with our deceased loved ones. For your information, I began to seriously enter the Transcendental Search during my early teens and continue to do so even as I'm writing to you. You guys have not yet experienced profound tragedy and are too busily immersed in your energetic youth and technological world to enter this domain. In order for you to adapt to the oncoming technological tsunami, however, I would urge you to begin for it's here to stay.

The way that cultures deal with this type of search and its mysteries is by establishing various forms of religion along with critical supporting rituals. There are number of ways to classify religion, but let's just deal with some of the great ones.

Hinduism: This is an ancient polytheistic religion with its roots and practice in India. It's primarily based on the universal suffering of life and ways to diminish and eventually eliminate it. One travels through reincarnation or metempsychosis by experiencing a series of new lives or stages called Karmas, sometimes hundreds, from an ant to an elephant, until one reaches a final, eternal suffer-less stage or Moksha. The nature of this afterlife is not quite clear. It's important to note that the use of detailed descriptive and analytic philosophical language with words, unlike in Christian theology, is generally absent in Eastern religions.

Buddhism: Gautama Buddha was basically a Hindu heretic who, however, also held on to the basic concept that life is suffering, but he principally stresses that desire is its main cause. Once more, though there is a final after-life stage of the eternal absence of suffering, the nature of it is not described clearly with words.

Confucianism: Kong-Zi, or Confucius, the latter name given to him by the Romans, believed, once more, that life is primarily a state of suffering, and there are rituals that must be followed to diminish it. His belief in the nature of the afterlife, like the others, is not clear. It's interesting to note that he, almost entirely alone, mourned the death of his mother over a three-year period. When asked by one of his disciples about the nature of an afterlife, he answered, "You do not understand not even life. How then can you understand death?"

Judaism: This is the first major monotheistic religion with a personal God, Yahweh, as its creator along with the belief in sin and evil. Though the elimination of suffering is not as explicit a tenet as in the Eastern religions, it certainly is addressed in different ways. Bottom line, if one sins, one suffers. Also, God causes suffering as a test of faith in Him as powerfully described in the book of Job. It's the rules of God such as the Ten Commandments or as in the Talmud along detailed quite complicated rituals that must be followed to receive God's help in life. On Yom Kippur, the holiest day of Judaism, one seeks repentance and God's forgiveness. Regarding an afterlife, in the past the Sadducees did not believe in an afterlife while the Pharisees did. Today, in different ways, this division still exists.

Christianity: Catholicism, your ostensible religion, is the first and largest of the Christian religions with over a billion followers. Its core doctrine is clear. Adam and Eve, who never had a belly button or in-laws, ate the forbidden fruit in the Garden of Eden, disobeying God's command that created original sin, which was passed on to all humanity and is the cause of universal suffering. Jesus Christ, part of the Holy Trinity, came to earth as the "sacrificial lamb" to personally absorb original sin and related human sins in order to open the doors for good people to enter the Kingdom of Heaven. There is a Heaven and a Hell and faith and prayer are necessary to reach Heaven but are no guarantee to avoid sin and suffering on earth.

There are many Protestant religions with different doctrines, but mostly all believing in the divinity of Jesus Christ and the reality of sin and suffering.

Islam: As with Catholicism, there are over a billion members. Jesus, though a good man, is not considered divine. As an aside, it's interesting to note that Mary, the mother of Jesus, is the only woman mentioned in the Quran. Though sin and suffering are part of the Muslim belief, a more pleasurable human approach to life is believed on earth as well in Heaven. In Hell there is a relative scale for suffering; the more you sin, the more you suffer.

Ersatz Religions: There are growing numbers of ersatz or independent "religious" groups springing up almost everywhere in our country that are not part of organized religions, and whose objective is to lighten the burdens of life by decreasing suffering and searching for things transcendental. Their beliefs and rituals sometimes overlap.

There are multiple small, single groups of churches with independent interpretations of the Bible, a large percentage being of Black or Hispanic cultures. I've attended a few of these churches and have been impressed by the energy manifested. You both attended one where I gave a talk about a deceased family friend, and you felt the robust energy of the people fueled by energetic music and song that permeated the vibrant service.

"Nones" are exploding among the young. They profess no religion and many are borderline agnostics or veering into spiritualism. The latter is difficult to define. Classically, it deals with communicating with the deceased or good and evil spirits. Not so today; and it's expressed in various ways depending on the mentality of the individual.

There is another interesting and growing movement among those attracted to the mystical Eastern religions. The current prevalent one is yoga, a Hinduism ritual. Classically, its purpose is to separate the soul from the mind and body in order to release one from the reincarnation cycle and finally reach Moksha or Nirvana where suffering is no more. But yoga has become much more Western and has developed into more practical objectives employing rituals to achieve peace of mind or tranquility in these hectic modern times and not at all related to ending reincarnation and suffering forevermore.

There's a rapidly growing movement that I call Entertainment Religion. Its primary ritual is based on rock concert-like formats to large audiences, frequently accompanied by strobe lights and excitatory musical techniques. Christian message songs are sung by the musicians on their "pulpits" and the people respond with rhythmic body movements. For more than one reason, I am personally intrigued by this ritual, one reason being that it reminds me of St. Augustine's observation that, "When one sings, one prays twice."

There are other major historic religions whose primary purpose was to appease and please major deities and not so much to relieve personal suffering. (I'm sure similar religions still exist on a smaller scale.) For example, in order to avoid famine and pestilence, the Aztec and Egyptian rituals included sacrificing humans from babies to the elderly to appease their Sun Gods whose necessary rays gave life to plant and animal life. The Druids not only practiced human sacrifice but also cannibalism.

Olivia and Stephen Carlos, you have seen how frequent physical and mental suffering coupled with daily and periodic transcendental searching are currently an integral part of the human condition in the traditional world. But we are now in the process of rapidly crossing the Rubicon entering the new world of disappearing tradition into that of the controlling technology one where the nature of and ways of handling suffering and searching will be changed—and, my grandchildren, they will be!

We'll first take a look at how the "broad" nature of sex and the existence of God are being persuasively altered, two critical forces in human behavior, before we get to the heart of the matter in the last chapter.

Now, my dear grandchildren, I'm about to take you into deeper depths of reality and truth, which may be tough for you to handle. I'll leave you with the following choices which are up to you to make:

Lasciate ogni speranza, voi ch'intrate: Dante's Divine Comedy
(Abandon all hope ye who enter here)
Abbiate ogni speranza voi ch'intrate: Grandpa's Option
(Have all hope ye who enter here)

Chapter 6

THE SURPRISE DYNAMICS OF THE SEXUAL REVOLUTION

"Sex is like fire: it can warm up your home or burn it down."
Grandpa

Sex is everywhere–more free than ever, profoundly impacting every walk of life from conception to the graveyard, or, increasingly, the crematorium. Chlamydia and pornography are now an integral expanding part of our culture with no end in sight. You frequently hear that we are living in what is commonly labeled as the sexual revolution era. Interestingly enough, however, to my knowledge, no one has sufficiently defined what sex is, including its extremely complicated dynamics that drive it. For instance, in physics there are four natural forces–gravity, electromagnetism, weak and strong nuclear ones, the latter two pertaining to the atom. Based on these forces, physicists can describe everything from what's behind the movement of celestial bodies to how to construct an atomic bomb.

Before I go on, let's take a look at a few examples on how sex can sometimes be a vicious and fatal venture in the animal kingdom as it is also with us humans. After all, we are animals.

The female praying mantis is much larger than the male. When mating time arrives, the male cautiously approaches the female, though knowing he's in mortal danger for the female loves to try to bite off his head while performing the sexual act. Unfortunately, most of the times he loses his head to her digestive system. We don't exactly know the reason behind this act, but do know the male speeds up his sexual performance after his decapitation which is a compelling explanation.

There was a television documentary regarding a male bison's preparatory ritual when he somehow senses when his honeybun will be receptive to having the sexual act. For about three months before the act the male's hormones begin to flow so much so that it even drives him to attack his potential male rivals. During this period of time he fights and sometimes kills his rivals, or is even killed himself. If he survives, battle-worn, he finally enters the herd to seek his lady bison mate. After having found her, he mounts her and within fifteen seconds he has his orgasm and releases his sperm and then walks away–forever!

I saw another documentary about the male lion. When the female is in heat and ready to accept the male, her sexual appetite is insatiable. It's estimated that she has hundreds of orgasms over a couple of days. During that time the male, mightily enjoying himself in the beginning, must service her calling upon all of his body's energy reserves. Now this is your grandfather's theory. I believe that many of the males croak from heart attacks either during the act or shortly thereafter, and the females know it. According to my theory, that is why there are far fewer male lions than there are female lions!

Stephen Carlos, I'm glad you're not a male praying mantis, bison or lion!

Now let's get on to the vastly more complicated human kingdom.

What's driving the sexual revolution is the exploding permissible freedom to experience the broad, inherent variety of mental and physical sexual properties which are being speedily propelled by advancing technology. Thus, there are robot talking companions of human size and surgical and/or hormonal treatments for transgender procedures. Gametes and embryos are routinely frozen and LGBTQ and other direct or indirect sexual acts are becoming increasingly acceptable and many are here to stay. Now both of you, never having been fully exposed to the traditional American culture before the '60s, may think that this revolution is normal. Not so. Not even close! This sudden freedom of sexual expression is a first-time historical movement. In all cultures sexual expressions have always been heavily regulated, either by law or custom, because of their actual or perceived dark or unacceptable downside.

To help you understand the etiology or cause behind the sexual revolution, I propose the Brain Genital Law or BGL which controls all the forces in the brain that send signals which awaken and stimulate the genitals, or the other way around, of both men and women making them at least think about, let alone pursue, the sexual act between a man and a woman, principally driven by the ultimate quest to achieve orgasms. And why is this? It deals with the obvious and primary purpose of evolution which is to propagate the race. If men and women don't make love there will be no babies and, therefore, no human race. Because of this inherent biologically-driven mandate to ensure its success, the brain, by necessity, is permeated with neurotransmitters and other types of signalers to mentally and physically stimulate the genitals of men and women but more, as we shall see, in the former. Thus the BGL forces are behind such manifestations as homosexuality, pedophilia, sodomy, cross-dressing, both mental and physical gender dysphoria, domination, submission, seduction, ménage a trois, perfume under the ears, the bong and marijuana, the tightest of leggings, male and female prostitution and snuff movies, among many others, all of which are intended to encourage the propagation of the race primarily, to repeat, by pursuing orgasms.

Now here's where I'm going to get into real big trouble with your parents and others, for they ain't going to like what I have to say. The BGL is, as with the forces of the physical world, a biologically natural, amoral law which exists in the brain. With the advances of modern technology and the soon-to-come highly effective disruptive aphrodisiacs for both men and women which now do not exist, unimaginable sexual expressions such as in the virtual space world, unimaginable both in number and types, will become commonplace. And, pay attention to this. They will become addictive! It is inevitable, and the negative consequences will be universal.

Why then, if it is natural, have there been—and still are—severe restrictions on the freedom of sexual expression in all worldwide cultures ranging from small tribes to larger, modern civilizations? Though the details of the origins of such regulations vary, what is clear is that they are, as I said before, based on the legitimate fear of the dark and vicious side of such sexual freedom.

But before we go on, and, at my age, before I forget, I have always been puzzled by our broad cultural ignorance of the biblical history of sex, probably because it has understandably been suppressed by religious leaders. And why, my grandchildren, is that so? Think about it. The voluminous Old Testament is saturated with histories of sexual escapades and prohibitions on many but not nearly all of them. In the New Testament there are few such stories, but there's a clear affirmation of obeying the Ten Commandments, which has its sexual prohibitions.

In the Book of Genesis, the first chapter in the Bible, after Adam and Eve ate the forbidden fruit which may have truly been sexual copulation because of the location of the fig leaves, such interpretation is rarely raised because the historic Judeo-Christian concern with the dark and downsides of sex. Then the first case of polygamy was reported when Lamech married two women, Adah and Zillah.

Other events such as sodomy and homosexuality were recorded when God destroys Sodom and Gomorrah because the men indulged themselves by practicing sodomy with other men. God sent to Lot, who was a good man and God-fearing guy who lived in Sodom, a male angel in order to encourage Lot to get out of town before God destroyed both cities. The men of Sodom somehow heard about the angel and wanted him for their own pleasure. Lot, would you believe, then offered his daughters to them as a substitute sexual partner, but the men refused. Lot then had no choice but to get out of town in a hurry before God, with a ball of fire, destroyed the entire city and its inhabitants. Unfortunately, his wife lost her life on the way for being too nosey.

Another biblical episode recounts the story of Abraham's wife, Sarah, and surrogate motherhood. She was way too old to conceive and have a baby, so Abraham chose to make love to his slave, Hagar, who then bore him a son.

Jumping ahead to the provocative Old Testament chapter, Deuteronomy, there are a number of warnings against men pursuing their sexual gratification of orgasms.

"Cursed is the man who sleeps with his father's wife…"

"Cursed is the man who sleeps with his sister…"

"Cursed is the man who sleeps with his mother-in-law..."

"Cursed is the man who has sexual relationships with animals..."

Now what is interesting to note is that women are not cursed if they sleep with their fathers, brothers, fathers-in-law or animals which puzzles me. On the other hand, in this chapter women do take a weird hit, which reasoning also puzzles me. It reads, "If two men are fighting and the wife of one of them comes to rescue her husband from his assailant, and reaches out and seizes him by his genitals, you shall cut off her hand. Show her no pity."

Bottom line, though some modern feminist groups for some reason choose to deny it, it's self-evident that men are far, far hornier than women. The superb actress, Julia Roberts, once said something like, "When a man has a naked woman in his bedroom he has won the lottery."

You may wonder about the origin of the word "horny." Well, there was a 17th century play entitled *The Country-Wife* written by William Wycherley. It's about a guy, Mr. Horner, who faked being a eunuch due to a pretended physical injury of his genitals in order to seduce married women. I'm not clear on why he wasn't attracted to unmarried ones. He started a business in his home selling chinaware in order to give a legitimate reason for married women to visit where he would seduce them–and the ladies were all for it! His physician, Dr. Quack, helped him spread the word around town that he was impotent and, therefore, the husbands need not worry when their wives were alone with him in his home ostensibly selling his wares. The sting was a huge success, and Mr. Horner made love to many women fooling their husbands, who sometimes were in the adjoining room in his home waiting to take their wives home. The guy's sexual appetite was insatiable, and this is how the word "horny" entered our vocabulary.

I mentioned in previous pages that, due in large part to advancing technology, the world between a man and a woman is rapidly narrowing. Regarding sexual activity, one huge dynamic reality is strangely absent in the public domain. It's the unequivocal fact that in sexual matters women are the flame and men are the moths. They are the attractive ones who rule the sexual roost and generally decide when to enter the bedroom. Now my grandchildren this will enrage much of our current female community despite the unequivocal fact that it's true. Women, therefore, have way more responsibility regarding the sexual act and should bear the price of that burden in various ways regarding judgmental situations.

Let me tell you a revealing story that happened not too long ago. There was the great heavyweight champion of the world, Mike Tyson, who allegedly raped a gal after she consented to visit with him in his hotel room. The gal then took him to court accusing him of rape which may or may not have happened. Though it was his word against hers, she won the case and the guy was sent to prison. Virtually the entire media, including male reporters, and feminist groups enthusiastically embraced the verdict, except the old-timer ladies in my old Italian neighborhood, including my mother, who was a very wise, strong and traditional woman yet, surprisingly, with women's liberation inclinations. One night in Philadelphia, I met with my mother and about a dozen old-timer women at a delightful Italian dinner reunion. Of course, the rule was that I would pay the bill, and none ever considered otherwise. So, what's new! That night, the wine flowed and the ladies were very much alive and in good form. They, very unfortunately, with their years of accumulated traditional wisdom, are a disappearing breed.

They ate their pasta and whatever else with enthusiasm while sipping on the Ruffino Chianti. It was a happy and upper group until the story of Mike Tyson came up, whereupon the mood of the ladies dramatically switched gears into the anger zone. One of the silver-haired ladies, obviously upset, boomed out, "What the hell was she doing in his hotel room, anyway? Did she expect him to ask her how she made her goddamn meatballs and wanted her recipe? She wasn't an innocent angel and must have known that he was probably a very horny guy and by the very fact she agreed to go to his room, he must have interpreted it as a green light to make whoopee. Why else would she go there?" The ladies all, in sync, nodded their heads in agreement. She should have known better. In other words, particularly with a tough guy growing up a tough neighborhood, she knew, as almost all women know, about the driving power behind the male orgasm and believed both of them should have shared the blame, if anything really did happen. Can you imagine these *grandes dames* debating this case on the television show, The View, with all those liberal women? It would be an historic event, to say the least, and I think the old-timers would have convincingly won the debate if there was an objective referee. And multi-millions of viewers would have not only thoroughly enjoyed the performance but have been reminded about the responsibility of women in the sexual act.

No matter what you have read or heard about, there is and never has been a true aphrodisiac. Since ancient times it has been principally men, you know, those horny creatures, who are on the eternal quest to stimulate the genitals not only to increase their sexual performance but also to powerfully increase sensual sensations before and during ejaculation. During the Middle Ages, for example, it was recommended that men consume three oysters–not more or less or they would not work!–as the aphrodisiac of choice on their honeymoon and to avoid consuming lettuce, a perceived sexual downer. Yes, some current recreational drugs do increase the sexual sensation but they are, for a number of obvious reasons, currently impractical such as mushrooms. There are now pharmaceutical drugs such as Viagra to treat erectile dysfunction in men, but they are not true aphrodisiacs.

A yet unrecognized and, I believe, a soon-to-arrive discovery will be the availability of a true aphrodisiac for both men and women. Now, when I mention the possibility of the availability of such an aphrodisiac, practically, all folks smile, including both of you, I bet, for mankind has been waiting for this pleasurable, treasured experience for a long time. Well, my grandchildren wipe that smile off your face for it will have catastrophic consequences because women will become as horny as men leading to cultural chaos unleashing the mighty force of the BGL and all kinds of destructive sexual activity. We already know that women and men can, due to spinal cord injuries, have multiple orgasms in a single day, an exhausting and disruptive psychological experience, and none is happy about it. The aphrodisiacs will inevitably not only lead to increased heterosexual acts but, as I just said, to mostly all others.

Imagine waking up in the morning with an aphrodisiac pill in your bathroom cabinet or a simple, stimulating medical device in the drawer. *It will become a daily temptation oftentimes resulting in some form of addiction and inevitably to pervasive cultural destabilization. Jealousy, hate, family disintegration, among others, will lead to increased government control.*

Chapter 7

PERSUASIVE EVIDENCE TO SUPPORT GOD'S EXISTENCE

Olivia and Stephen Carlos, I want you to know up front that this is not a chapter on religion, which many at your age would react as a turn-off subject simply because they are not that interested in it. It basically deals with the evidence that supports the existence of a personal God which is the *sine qua non* foundation for the Judeo-Christian religion. *If you remove the existence of God, then religion based on faith in a God obviously make no sense.* And this is precisely what's happening in Western cultures, and it's gaining speed. The belief in the existence of a personal God is currently no match for the anti-God technology-driven secularism and Scientism, the belief that the use of the scientific method is the only way to arrive at absolute truth. And, for reasons that puzzle the hell out of me, our religious leaders do not perceive the dynamics behind this anti-God movement. God and prayer are being driven out of our daily discourse from kindergarten to the universities, even Christian ones.

Now why, you may ask, am I alarmed at this ongoing phenomenon? It's simple. Despite its many historic letdowns, the Judeo-Christian based religions have effectively promoted reliable good behavior from the critical importance of the family to general good deeds. Even the atheist, Voltaire, believed that even if God doesn't exist, we must establish his existence in order to promote the good and minimize the bad in all of us. Remember the Six Human Characteristics? *Now if you eliminate a major force which controls human behavior another force will take its place.* For example, Alcoholics Anonymous helps its members replace their dependence on alcohol by replacing it with the belief in a loving personal God or other replacements.

Today, our thought leaders are replacing God's guidance to human behavior with the moral-ethical approach. Before I go on, much of the latter approach is based on the erroneous belief in the natural existence of human rights. Though I hate to tell you this, there isn't such an entity. You only have a right depending on where you are at a point in time. Just ask the Muslims in China versus those in Iran today.

What then are the definitions and foundations of moral and ethical, and what's the difference between the two? Why not give it a try? You will discover that they are very vague and imprecise. Yet these two words are frequently employed to add to the misleading profundity of someone's message. How often do you hear or read something akin to, "This is a serious moral and ethical issue that must be resolved."?

Let me propose a working definition and also give you one example. Morality proposes the existence of a broad principle of good behavior and ethical deals with how to apply it. It's similar to when Congress proposes a law and the government regulators fill in the complicated details on how to apply it. An example of a moral principle is, "Do not tell a lie" that traditional parents teach their kids. The ethicist takes this moral principle and applies it to real-life situations. Let's say caring parents with a very limited income cheat on their income taxes, which is telling a lie, in order to send their child to a vocational school or college. This would be considered an unethical act by the ethicists, but to normal, hard-working folks it would be an understandable and "good" or ethical act. Whose side would you take? If, however, wealthy parents cheat on their taxes that would clearly be considered unethical. But hold your horses! Some believe it may not be so for government wastes their taxes and yes, even on some unethical acts.

Here's a more provocative example: It's torture, the use of means to substantially increase pain and suffering to get one to confess or for other objectives. Words such as torture and racism evoke such an eruptive, emotional reaction that is totally immune to reason. The use of torture came under intense attacks after 9/11, the destruction of the Twin Towers, by, who else?–the enemy. Attempts by the government to employ torture to find out who was behind it and also to discover what and where future attacks on America would happen were themselves severely attacked by our thought leaders as immoral and broadly supported by the media.

If, you had the opportunity to torture a man before the attack who knew it would happen, like the Germans did with the Italians and the hot poker, what would be the moral or ethical thing to do? What would you do? Confusing, isn't it? But not for me!

Now let's take a look at the philosophical-theological and scientific anti-God arguments which are being extremely effectively employed by the agnostic and atheistic thought leaders particularly targeted at the younger population. *You will see that with the help of your Emoji brains that these arguments are actually icons which support the existence not only of God but of a personal one.*

First of all what's the difference between philosophy and theology? Philosophers use reason and other methods to analyze various subject matter such as morality and epistemology, without generally dealing with religious issues. Theologians frequently use the same methods, but broaden the subject matter to include religious subject matter such as the interpretation of the Bible. Did God create the heavens and earth, and what is the nature of the Holy Trinity?

The men, and they are mostly men, in both fields are an interesting group. I met the first one in my first philosophy course in college. I'll never forget the guy for he was an eccentric-looking creature, to say the least, but a superb teacher, the kind who gets your mind out of the rut of daily routine thinking. It was on the first day of my course when he asked the class why did the great Greek civilization arise? He quizzed a number of students and pointed out how their explanations were woefully inadequate. I was hoping that he would shut down the quiz before he got to me, but it was a vain hope. He, frequently pulling on his nose with his right hand, walked next to my desk and asked, "Mr. DeFelice, what do you think about the reason or reasons?" I, without hesitation, answered, "I haven't the slightest idea. It's an impossible question to answer." He smiled, lightly, gently patted the back of my head and said, "You are correct young man, and you are an honest man with an honest intellect." Though I was somewhat pleased to hear the compliment, I truly didn't understand why he made it. After all, all that I said was that I didn't know.

As the course went on, we tackled subject matter such as what is truth and what's the proper structure of government. It struck me like a thunderbolt that there were many theories but unlike in mathematics, there was clearly no general agreement among philosophers on many fundamental issues. Later on in my readings, I came to the same conclusion about theologians. One evening while having a martini with my friend and colleague, Patricia Park, and Turner Catledge, the former managing editor of the New York Times who was on my foundation board, I came up with the idea of raising a couple of million dollars to gather the top philosophers and theologians in a huge conference room where I would lead the discussion to see if I could get them to unanimously agree on a single major subject such as whether they, themselves, existed or not. Don't laugh for I'm not kidding.

One of history's greatest philosophers and currently very influential in academic circles, Scottish David Hume, thought a lot about epistemology doubting, for example, that we cannot really know that much about cause and effect. One day he declared, "Certitude is for fools," which got me thinking whether it applied to his own philosophy. It's said that on another day while he was playing billiards with a friend, he panicked, doubting his own existence and pleaded with his friend to prove that he was wrong.

It's always important to have some understanding behind the human characteristics of thought leaders for it helps you understand what motivates them.

First of all, philosophers and theologians love to think. In fact, I would call it their major occupation. Also they usually, but not always, do so in what I call Within Group Think where they try to out-think the intellectual group competition. I'm not criticizing this quality, but applaud it. Competition sparks creativity. The downside, however, it limits their scope of subject matter.

One characteristic that got me thinking when I was a student was that few of them never ran or run a business where the principal challenge is to survive in the real world. Businessmen and women deal with and handle real-life people many of whom are difficult to handle and real pains-in-the-ass. Also, they must outsmart their competition not only to stay in business but to survive. In a real sense, it's dog-eat-dog. Olivia, you got your part-time job in the service business a couple of years ago and told me how difficult people can sometimes be.

Those philosophers and theologians who are professors at universities where most of them work, fight, as teachers do with the help of unions, to obtain tenure or job security where they cannot be fired for incompetency. If, however, you are an incompetent in business you go out of business. The business owner, therefore, is more motivated to be more knowledgeable about what drives human behavior as well as more competent than a professor or teacher. Is this a negative comment? If I were a professor, I would do the same thing as they do for job security and self-interest is a critical key to living well enough. It all depends how you look at it. What do you think?

Now I know what you're thinking. Does this mandated security result into a general national state of poor educational instruction? A tough question to precisely answer, but, for reasons of personal experience and other searches, I'm optimistic. Both of you told me that you like your teachers, except for only a couple of bad eggs, which hopefully supports my optimism.

There is another characteristic of philosophers and theologians, except for highly religious ones, which is their historic avoidance to deeply deal with such subjects as human love and traditional marriage. I often wonder why, and I don't have an answer. What do you think? These subjects had been largely relegated to novelists, poets and therapists. But during the last half of the last century the subject of sex and the subtle beginnings of the sexual revolution and current LGBTQ, lesbian, gay, bisexual, transgender and queer, began. Michel Foucault, a gay philosopher who died of AIDS, wrote the voluminous *History of Sexuality,* favoring the freedom of sexual expression similar to the BGL but with few brakes on such expression! Today, sparked by the Internet, all types of thoughtful as well as horse's ass parties have entered this realm but are largely coldly clinical lacking romance and beauty which reflects the general face of the coldness of our present-day culture.

Before I go on, there's a habit I developed while in medical school when, in addition to medicine, I not only studied the various viewpoints of philosophers and theologians but also about their personal life behavior which, to repeat, really adds to their profile of behavior and thought. In addition, it's interesting reading, and you should develop this habit of taking a brief look at the life some of these folks. It adds to the pleasure of learning. Take the Greek Cynic philosopher, Diogenes. He lived in a barrel in public and carried around a lighted lantern during the day. When asked why, he answered, "I'm searching for an honest man."

Centuries later there was the brilliant Catholic theologian, Origen, who was assigned to teach a class of women. Evidently, he was a very horny man and, therefore, highly concerned with his chastity and literally interpreted Jesus's parable in Matthew of the New Testament that, "... there be eunuchs which have made themselves eunuchs for the kingdom of heaven's sake." So he castrated himself in order to suppress his sexual appetite before teaching the women's class. He was such a great theologian to earn him the right to be canonized by the Catholic Church as a saint, but he was denied this honor because it's written in Deuteronomy of the Old Testament that, "No man whose testicles have been crushed or whose organ has been removed shall become a member of the assembly of the Lord."

Now let's proceed to the philosophical-theological and scientific arguments regarding the existence of a personal God. *Pay particular attention to this for, as I told you before, your teachers will tell you that they do not support such an existence when they clearly do.* Why is that? Keep reading, and you decide.

THE PHILOSOPHICAL-THEOLOGICAL ARGUMENTS

The "big three" arguments, though there is inevitable overlapping, are categorized as ontological, cosmological and teleological.

The ontological argument simply proposes that the idea of a Supreme Being is somehow inherently in the human brain. St. Anselm, who was an Italian who somehow became the Archbishop of Canterbury during the Middle Ages, proposed that since the brain or mind can think about an entity as great as God which is beyond the brain's capacity to think on that level, this Entity, therefore, must exist. Descartes, who is considered the founder of modern philosophy, has another theory why the idea of God is in the human brain. Unlike Anselm who proposed that the searching mind is the reason, Descartes proposes that God, himself, places the idea in it.

It's important to note that their entire arguments are much more complex than my summary but the overviews are sound.

Now to the cosmological argument proposed by Aristotle which primarily deals with change and what causes change. But before we get to his argument, let's take a look at two previous philosophers, Heraclitus and Parmenides, who also were interested in the concept of change. Heraclitus said that everything changes, and Parmenides said that nothing changes. The following is a challenging riddle that I want you to think about and then make a conclusion. Heraclitus would claim that, if you dunked your foot in a river, then removed it and then dunked it again, it's a different river. Parmenides would tell Heraclitus that he's full of baloney for it's the same damn river. Who would you agree with? Or can it be both? Not easy, is it?

Getting back to the incomparable Aristotle: He maintains that all things at a point in time are changing and, therefore, something unchangeable must be the cause that's causing all these changes. This uncaused cause or prime mover, another term, he called god, an intelligent entity. This god, of course, is not a personal one but some type of cosmic force. The great Catholic theologian, St. Thomas Aquinas, used this argument, as one of his five arguments, as evidence for the existence of a personal God. This persuasive Aristotelean argument may not hit you up front but requires some serious thought. So put yourselves in a dark, quiet place, turn on a Beethoven sonata and cogitate until the revelation arrives. If not, give me a call!

Now to teleology and, once more, to our unescapable friend, Aristotle. He argued that everything exists for a purpose which infers that something intended these acts to happen for a purpose. For example, water exists so there can be life. Aquinas takes this to a higher level, arguing that since all things in nature have a purpose or intent then there must be a supreme intelligence to have created all the governing forces which make it happen. And, it logically follows that this intelligent being is a personal God.

The most famous and often-attacked analogy supporting the teleological argument was effectively promoted by the English clergyman theologian, William Paley, in his book, *Natural Theology*, published in

1802. In it he compares a watch to the world and the watchmaker, the entity who made the watch, to an intelligent personal God. If you were walking in a field and came upon a watch on the ground what would you think about it? First, some person lost the watch. It just wasn't there on its own. Then if you took it apart, you would discover how all the complex integral parts were intentionally designed and assembled by someone for the purpose or intent of recording the time. As an analogy, Paley argued, nature is also a complex structure with multiple functions, and it logically follows that there must be a transcendent, intelligent watchmaker or designer who, he concludes, is a personal intelligent God.

The argument is quite persuasive to most men and women, but lots of philosophers and others, particularly, those who are not sympathetic to God's existence, have been energized, using words, to discredit its rationale. Let's take a look at another analogy. If you and a philosopher were walking in a field and came upon a Tootsie Roll or Nutella Bar on the ground, you would conclude that someone in a specific company conceived of its content and how to produce it. What would the philosopher say? He'd say that nature is not a man-made Tootsie Roll and, therefore, no supreme maker is necessary.

Now pay particular attention to what I have to say for it will apply to much of your future education. All of the aforementioned arguments can be declared faulty by philosophers, even Christian ones, by the attempted use of reason employing, as always, the faulty use of words. But so can their own arguments! So where does that leave us? It leads us to the Emoji brain. Take for example the watchmaker argument, from the existence of the watchmaker of the watch to the watchmaker of nature. Your Emoji brains, not your attempts at the use of words and reason, based on a lifetime of icon observations from the small to the large, will lead you to comfortably conclude that there must be a watchmaker for all of nature and that watchmaker must have an intelligence to both create and program the purposes of its parts. If not, what else can it be? Think about it. Now let us visit the subject of science which, in grandpa's opinion, also supports the existence of a personal God.

Is this chapter getting too heavy? Pay attention and hang in there, for it's more important than you think.

SCIENCE: THE BIG BANG, EVOLUTION AND
GRANDPA'S HUMAN SIGNALER

The Big Bang: It's estimated that the universe was created about 14.6 billion years ago in a trillionth of a trillionth of a second, tough to conceive, from a small particle no bigger than the period at the end of this sentence. The existence of this particle was first predicted by the Belgian priest, Georges Lemaitre, in 1927. He called it the Cosmic Egg. Now think about this mind-blowing fact. Every atom and everything that exists since then from the billions of immense galaxies to your tiny selves and also your grandfather was contained in this tiny, material particle. Everything! What really fascinates me and gets me thinking is that it formed the human brain that has immaterial thoughts. How can the immaterial come from the material? Think about this. Surprisingly, this mysterious phenomenon is rarely seriously openly addressed. Ask yourselves why.

Let's think about the following questions that deserve to be addressed if one is to be intellectually honest which, by the way, is not that common as we shall see:

- What is the Cosmic Egg? What could this thing be made of to be able to create every existing atom in the universe?
- What made the Cosmic Egg? Did it exist eternally or not?
- What could have caused the Big Bang to happen? This is a simple matter of cause and effect.
- Where and what is the universe heading into? The universe is expanding faster than the speed of light and heading into something. What is that something? Infinity? Can you imagine coming to the end of something and not being able to take another step forward? But, also, can you imagine our universe or others not coming to an end?

    You will be surprised to know that our thought leaders have almost completely avoided addressing these questions. Pause here, and ask yourselves why. I'd like you, at this point, to concentrate on Question 3 for it deals with the act of creation. One can view such creation in two ways. The first is to bring something into existence from nothing and the second is to expand the existence of something or from something else. Now your Emoji brain tells you that some entity had to create the Cosmic Egg and something had to create the Big Bang to release its potential contents. Now I want to re-emphasize that the act of creation led to two mysterious phenomena—the creation of both physical and immaterial or non-physical entities. Regarding the latter, we are dealing with the brain or mind with intelligence that thinks, analyzes, plans, wonders and executes acts, among other properties. And there's nothing in the world of physics that can remotely explain the causes behind the forces that created these two phenomena. Nothing at all, but it's one of the best kept secrets of them being ignored.

So what other possible explanation is there? One is the Bible and the Book of Genesis. It begins, "In the beginning God created the heaven and the earth." Then it says, "God created man in his own image in the image of God he created him; male and female he created them."

Now both of you know that I'm not a religious man and not pushing to prove the Biblical God's existence, but simply to consider it like the entity that I proposed in the God chapter, particularly since there is no other reasonable option yet proposed.

Before I go on, I'd like to alert you to future encounters that may be confusing but are not relevant to the subject of God as objectively presented in this book.

I have a good, wise and kind friend who is a distinguished lawyer and long-time agnostic. He had lost his wife and daughter, as I had happen to me, within a very short period of time, and was bereft with sadness and understandable anger. One day while we were having a tasty Paella Valencia along with a solid Spanish white wine served at the right temperature, he, with passion, asked me the very legitimate question on how can a God who is good, permit so much suffering and misery in this world. I, of course, had no answer. Nobody does.

I want to point out that you may come across questions like this in the future, but these are religious ones and are, to repeat, not the subject of this book.

FYI, I have a hunch that some agnostics are deep-down atheists who are afraid to admit it even to themselves for fear they may be wrong and that a Hell might indeed exist. And I don't blame them!

Now to the highly controversial subject of Evolution: Darwinism, the concept of evolution, shared by Charles Darwin and Alfred Russell Wallace, is the major force that you will be taught by your teachers and professors, among others, that evolution finally puts the nail in the coffin of any belief that God plays a role in the creation of life. Its teaching remains a major tool of the anti-God thought leaders. Though there are some variations, its basic tenet is that the development of the plant and animal kingdom, including we humans, occurs by random genetic mutation and the environment in which it occurs which directs the evolutionary process.

Now there's no doubt that evolution occurred and is ongoing, but Darwinism, as a fact, has its serious flaws. First of all, there's the Ramsey theorem which demonstrates that complete patternlessness or randomness is impossible. Then there's the rather recent emergence of the field of epigenetics in which the environment, either within or outside the body, can impact gene expression without altering the structure of the gene or genetic mutation. Thus methylation can alter the expression of certain genes and elevated temperatures can change the determination of sexual gender in certain animals. And finally, Darwinism does not explain the origin of life.

Now catch this. The unquestionably brilliant aspects of Darwinism deal only with the parts of the process of life and not with its origins and other phenomena. A more comprehensive view deals with what I call **The Mysterious Six Phases of Life.** They are as follows:

The first is abiogenesis: How did animate or living matter originate from inanimate or non-living matter?

The second is self-replication: How did RNA and DNA self-replicate themselves, let alone come to be?

The third is self-organization: How did this living matter organize itself in order to function, thrive and stay alive?

The fourth, not to be confused with the second, is emerging phenomena: How did simple organisms develop more complicated and sophisticated organ systems? How, for example, did the human brain evolve from a more primitive phase of evolution such as prokaryotes, single-cell organisms without a nucleus?

***The fifth: The existence of consciousness*:** I personally consider the mystery of consciousness, the act of being aware of oneself, the most interesting of all. It's the threshold to most of life's experiences from awakening to awakening with dreams in between.

***The sixth: The existence of the human mind*:** Its existence is clearly a quantum jump in the evolutionary process separating humans from the rest of living creatures. We are not even sure whether it's strictly located in the brain or throughout the body. Examples of some of the mind's mind-boggling feelings and functions are: consciousness, recognition, recall, altruism, schadenfreude, love of many types, hate of many types, sadness, thought, analysis, happiness, submission, domination, optimism, thought, jealousy, curiosity, phobias, envy, reasoning, rationalization, optimism, friendship, loyalty, patriotism, depression, anxiety, ambition, submission, aggression, friendship, creativity, spiritualism, transcendental searching, making judgements in all walks of life from planning a wedding to ways of constructing weapons of mass destruction.

Conclusion: The weight of evidence of ***The Six Mysteries*** cannot be based on Darwinism. And before I forget, you should remember that all of the mysteries are intended to have a purpose!

GRANDPA'S HUMAN SIGNALER

Olivia and Stephen Carlos, I'd like you to pay particular attention to your grandfather's attempt to use human signaling in order to accommodate the talented advocates of Scientism, the need to objectively quantify things by mainly using the scientific method. I wrote an open letter to Pope Francis right after his election and more recently, a more detailed, lengthy analysis of human signaling which is not appropriate for this book. But this very brief presentation of a few examples should take you to Beethoven's sonatas once more to make you ponder and wonder, two great pleasures of life.

Also, a warning is in order. I was, like Benjamin Franklin, a lousy student in mathematics, yet I did most of the calculations myself. So if you want, do some fact checking!

Signaling simply means that something happens by something making it happen. This something in a human being is called a signal. You will see that there are trillions and trillions of human signals that not only happen at a single point in time but for a lifetime–the purpose of which is to make you live. *It's critical to note that not only do these mega millions of life sustaining signals exist, but they are interconnected and synchronized to make it happen.* Another great mystery, regarding numbers, I want to shake up your minds in order to appreciate the immensity of the numbers we are dealing with, for we have become immune to them. We speak today, for example, of billions and trillions of dollars being spent by our government without giving it a second thought and not appreciating the enormity and magnitude of them. Now suppose your computers were hacked 100 times in a single day. You would say to yourselves, "Wow, that's not only incredible, but it's impossible to happen so many times." Your reactions to the following numbers should be even more mind expanding.

Let's start with those three pounds of flesh–I'll repeat, only three pounds of flesh–called the brain, the most marvelous and mysterious entity in existence. It's about the same weight as an Easter ham! There are a little less than 100 billion neurons or nerve cells which connect to each other through synapses in order to send all kinds of signals for all kind of activity. Some estimate that there are at least 10 trillion synapses, all in action or ready for action at a single point in time. There are three types of other cells, microglia, astrocytes and oligodendrocytes, at total of 300 billion of them, which support the billions of neurons.

The total number of brain cells, 400,000 billion of them, need water and electricity to function and send signals which, when both combined, amount to 800, 000 billion cellular presences. The brain contains arteries to carry oxygen and nutrients to its cells. I couldn't find any numbers regarding them, but they are, let's say, astronomical. *All the aforementioned are functioning sending signals at a point in time!*

Now let's take a look at the total body. It's estimated that there are 10 trillion cells in the body, all of which send signals at a point in time and for a lifetime. Though there are more, let's assume there are 20,000 genes in each cell. These genes send an untold number of signals, but let's assume an absurdly low number of 1,000 which amounts to 200,000,000 trillion signals at a single point in time!

If you're beginning to appreciate these numbers wait until you take a closer look at methylation: There is a chemical unit composed of carbon and hydrogen whose principal function is to keep the cell's molecules such as proteins, DNA and neurotransmitters, functioning normally. Sometimes they fail in their missions which results in some serious diseases. It's estimated that the body's methylation processes occur close to one billion times per second and in just one minute, 60 billion times.

Now here's a signaling function on which I'd like you do the mathematics. ATP is converted to ADP in the 10 trillion cell's mitochondria to produce energy and converted back to ATP. This process occurs three times per minute. What do you come up with?

Now, instead at a point in time, let's take a look at one example of annual signaling numbers because you are understandably beginning to lose interest for you already got the numbers point, but pay particular attention to this. There are 31,536,000 seconds in a year. Let's assume we are talking about the life span of 70 years. It was mentioned that there are about one billion methylation signals going on each second. One billion x annual seconds x70 equals 2,207,520,000,000,000,000 signals! Imagine adding up the trillions of total body signals over a lifetime.

Olivia and Stephen Carlos, I've only covered the tip of the tip of the tip of the iceberg. The total body signaling numbers are beyond mathematics, computational modeling and human comprehension. Interestingly enough, I spoke to a few very bright scientists and mathematicians, and they all agree there are no answers to what's making these signals happen. So why the general silence of these professionals?, for it ain't due to a lack of imagination. Something to think about, isn't it?

So what's the big story? Can these mega-trillions of signaling events happen by random mutations and chance alone without a unifying force to interconnect and synchronize them to make them work in harmony? Of course not! Do all the cells in the body work independently by themselves, accidently bringing about the primary purpose of a human, which is to live? Of course not! Emoji brain or not, there's not the slightest possibility of the aforementioned. There has to be some type of intelligence behind the unifying principle to bring all the signaling forces together. And I call this force *Grandpa's Human Signaler.*

THE EMOJI BRAIN AND PERSONAL GOD

To refresh your memory regarding the Emoji brain: The brain itself largely perceives life's events of all types as Emoji icons. It receives, stores, analyzes and judges such events not dependent on the use of words. You recall how the brain judges what a dingbat and horse's ass are and also how to distinguish between the two without saying a word.

How would it judge putting all categories together, let alone each separate category, the discussion on philosophers, the Big Bang, Evolution, the Six Mysteries and the Human Signaler? Would it conclude that these all occur by random, undirected happenings, or by some entity or cause behind their existence? The Emoji brain will conclude that not only each category, but their combination is unequivocally driven by a personal intelligent entity causing these effects. And one option is a personal God or at least an intelligent Transcendental Being.

Remember, this is a solid conceivable option and an honest anti-God thought leader would agree, only, however, if you corner him or her!

Chapter 8

WHAT'S GOING ON?

My grandchildren, the battle between the tradition and technology worlds is well on its way. I'm about to take you on an unsettling journey that few have traveled regarding what technology is and where it is taking us. The journey will cover where we currently are in our country covering the family, religion and sex, the broader and hidden message of the socialism movement, the future of the world and how you can adapt to it.

To refresh your memories, let's review the Six Human Characteristics: self-interest, self-deception, recognition, power-money, competition and altruism. Also, remember that all are constantly operational and the clear winner of the net effects of these characteristics regarding good versus evil is evil. Now, the state or government has the same characteristics as the human ones. Plato put it well when he said the state is the macrocosm of the microcosm of its people. Governments, therefore, are fundamentally evil. For that reason, we have laws and customs to suppress such evil. And the technology-driven evil will eventually win the day controlling all by driving out our traditional culture unless we do something about it.

Before I go on, I want to emphasize some key human personality traits that you should make a habit to keep in mind. The first, as I mentioned before and want to re-emphasize, is that increasingly, on many issues, you generally cannot please or make people receptive to your opinions. For example, if I say that racism is way overrated today, many, without analyzing my reasoning, would immediately emotionally conclude that I'm a racist. If, however, I say that racism is much more prevalent than generally realized, the immediate emotional response would be the same but by parties of the opposite belief. Both of these responses are classic examples of self-interest and self-deception.

Now the following of what I have to say will cause a deluge of Internet-generated hate. It deals with what the stevedore philosopher, Eric Hoffer, once proposed. As I said before, our country, the United States of America, is overwhelmingly unique in the enormous numbers of charitable organizations and individuals backed by men and women of abundant good will. But this, unfortunately, does not generally apply to the subjects such as racism, gender and diversity, among others. Hoffer made his observation regarding organizations in general, but it certainly holds true with some of the aforementioned ones. He said something like, "Many organizations begin as a cause, and then become a business and eventually a racket taking advantage of people and the society." They are classic examples of self-interest, self-deception and the quest for power and money. Imagine the fuming hatred that will follow after they read this.

Olivia and Stephen Carlos, bottom line, take careful note that much of what I have to say in the remaining pages of this book will be met with gut emotions of hatred instead of honest deliberation and reasoning.

THE FAMILY AND RELIGION

Family and religion are traditionally intertwined and serve largely as custodians of the values of a culture. In my youth love of country, patriotism and thriving religious institutions were commonplace. Both institutions now are rapidly being fractured leading to unstoppable changes primarily due to technology. Let's start with the disappearing traditional family.

About four decades ago, I was watching a television show with Grandma DeFelice, where the host asked the young man what his name was. He responded, "Joe." I was waiting to hear his last name but the young man never offered, and the host never asked which, for some reason, struck my curiosity. Then over time the last name, that which identifies your family, largely disappeared not only during introductions but in much of our culture. Now if you visit the doctor's or other offices your social security number or date of birth is asked in order to locate your records on the computer. You have become a cold cultural technological number. And no one seems to object or even care.

Right about then, two other phenomena occurred. Instead of traditionally assuming the family name of the husband, the wives either maintained their own last names independently or combined it, as in certain countries, with the husband's. About the same time divorce began to become increasingly common where today it is oftentimes expected to occur even, I hate to say, in the minds of newlyweds walking down the aisle. So let's assume a newlywed couple decided to keep both the last names of Mr. and Mrs. Jones Smith. Then they get a divorce and let's say the woman remarries a man with the last name of Peter Paul and then have a male child. What then is the child's name? Then years later he marries a young lady from divorced parents with a double last name. Who pays the price? Certainly the children!

Now here's something to think about. The legendary TV host, Larry King, who, a victim of Covid, just passed away, was divorced eight times, and I wonder what names his children bear. Speaking of King, he was interviewed once and was asked what was the saddest moment in his life. He replied that it was the death of his father. He was then asked what his second saddest moment was. His reply? The baseball homerun hit by Bobby Thomson which is known as, "The Shot Heard Around the World." Now Bobby was my friend, and when I told him about King's remark, he smiled broadly and warmly. I did meet Mr. King at dinner one night at a Friar's Club event and asked him whether he still held to his statement. He, sporting a serious demeanor, answered, "You bet!"

Let's look at another technological innovation that has contributed to the fading of the traditional family. It's the invention of the steam engine first used in trains in the mid-nineteenth century! This engine was the first mechanical technology which could move heavy objects without the use of manpower. Instead of a horse-driven stagecoach, it permitted people to travel great distances more easily and comfortably. It eventually sparked the discovery of all kinds of inventions such as the automobile and huge jet airplanes, which have led to unlimited mobility to travel to the farthest corners of the earth.

Remember that I told you that my family emigrated from Italy after World War I and settled in an old Italian neighborhood in Philadelphia.

All my aunts, uncles and cousins lived there within a stone's throw of each other. My grandmother was a severe diabetic requiring daily doses of insulin injections. My father, Stefano, your great grandfather, couldn't stomach delivering the injections so my Uncle Jimmy, after a hard-working day, dropped by to deliver the injections. When occasionally something went wrong in our home such as a broken railing, my Uncle Benny came over on the weekends to do the repairs.

The message is that families frequently helped families when in need because they lived close by. Also, money was saved by not having to pay a repairman.

Now look at your grandfather's situation who lives in an aging, large home. You live about an hour away, and your family calendar is thrombosed with daily activities. My only other close relative is your first cousin, or my first grandchild, Max, who is a strong young man, almost 30 years old. The only problem is that he lives in Florida! He visits his wife Tara's sister in New Jersey about twice a year and spends a single night with me, not much time to help out. They have two young daughters, Brielle and Kinsley, and a third daughter on the way, so I will have three great granddaughters in faraway Florida. Bottom line and as you will see with my friend, Christina, there are no relatives to help out. I must seek it elsewhere and, of course, at an emotional and monetary price.

Christina is in her nineties and lives alone in Manhattan with a periodic visiting helper. And, of course, at that age, she has her significant infirmities. She has three children, all good people, along with her grandchildren. One child lives in the northern part of our country; the other in the southern part and the other way out west. She has no one to rely on except her paid helpers, which help is quite limited. Yes, when she's really sick, one of her children comes to help out for a few days or more and quickly return to their homes. To be sure, the entire family comes to see her for Christmas for less than a week. Big deal!

How then does she communicate with her family when she's alone? It's Zooming. Zoom, spurred on by Covid, has become commonplace for millions of Americans to communicate not only with the family but with friends and others. The traditional family is being rapidly replaced with the technology-driven Zoom Family. And it's happening in your home. Your beautiful, kind Mexican mother regularly communicates with her

DeDios family in Mexico by Zoom or Smartphone, along with some of her siblings, who also live in America.

Now close the doors in your room, shut down your mind-controlling technology and just imagine being alone without being in and sensing the physical presence of others, the critical human condition for interpersonal communication. No touch, no hug, no kiss, no talking to each other, no Emoji brain silent icons such as observing the body language of physical pain and depression of your mother and father calling out for help, no general feeling of familial love–NO NOTHING!

Let's take a brief look at some other traditional family-destructive forces going on starting with the working mother and, *caveat emptor,* for here we go again! What I'm about to say will be interpreted by many as an anti-working mother diatribe when in fact it's just a mere description of what's going on. We are having a cultural nervous breakdown!

A number of decades ago it dawned on me that the references to the beauty of stay-at-home-mothers was disappearing, being replaced by stories and accolades of working and career mothers. The word "housewife" now has pejorative connotations. Traditionally, mothers are the glue that binds the family. They guide the family though life's inevitable trials and tribulations. Remember that they have a greater and more enduring capacity of love and sacrifice than fathers. By the very well-known fact that the men who are seriously wounded and dying on the battlefields of war cry out to their mothers, and not their fathers, is enough to prove the obvious point. So, what's going on today? For a variety of reasons, such as the need to maintain a higher quality of living by both husband and wife working to earn enough money, or to reach out to new technology-based experiences, many mothers today have full-time jobs. They must commute daily, oftentimes entailing lengthy journeys, to the workplace and back home. By the time they return home, they are understandably tired and understandably not up to handling traditional motherly functions. Can the father step in and help? It's going on now–but remember, my grandchildren, despite what you're taught, a father is not a mother!

Now here's an historic fact that, would you believe, I've never heard addressed. Housewives are frequently managers of the family overseeing and guiding what transpires from dawn to dusk. Going back to my childhood, I remember all but one of my aunts controlled the household.

And I've observed this up to today. Compare this to a mother at work sitting behind her computer all day, every day with eyes fixed on a screen and a total lack of body movement. Which is more boring, challenging and exhausting? Behind a computer all day or managing a family?

Now don't get me wrong. There are many moms, even with economic security, who prefer their jobs and careers rather than staying home. On the other hand, I know many more moms who are economically secure who much prefer to stay at home. I just raise this issue for educational purposes since you won't hear about it elsewhere. Why do you think this is so?

FYI, my wife, your grandmother, who left us before you got to know her, was a superb manager of our home and family yet managed to have a life of her own. But, as with many mothers, she was frequently over budget! You missed knowing a beautiful and wise woman.

The sexual revolution and the anti-God movement are two other family- destructive phenomena that I previously mentioned but I will add a few more points.

Remember when I pointed out that men were much hornier than women and that up to the sexual revolution this powerful drive played a major role in getting married. There was little sex outside of marriage. Shacking-up, an old term which I like, or living together without being married, was forbidden. So also was having sex when not living together. Now shacking-up is increasingly commonplace where, marriage and having children are being postponed or even totally abandoned because, in part, men now can have sex without the obligations of marriage as well as not having to go through painful now common divorce proceedings if things don't go well. The same, of course, with women.

During the past few years, I've taken an informal survey of quite a number of shacking-up men and women regarding why they were doing it. An almost universal response from men was that their experiences with married couples were that they were painful, unhappy relationships, and they needed that like a hole in the head. Now my take on my discussions with women was, which will upset certain women's groups, that it was okay in the beginning but as time rolled by, and if the economics were secure enough, they wanted marriage. They employ the great gift of feminine persuasion, but in my survey most have not yet tied the knot. A growing percentage of them are freezing their eggs waiting for the right moment to occur, usually that of marriage. Olivia and Stephen Carlos, let's discuss freezing your gametes for it's more complicated and risky than is generally known.

Bottom line, shacking-up is another growing force bringing about the demise of the traditional family. As Shakespeare wrote "Chastity tis a cold companion," and the sexual revolution attests to this wise man's observation.

And one final thought which will really disturb lots of women and even men: the general pattern of postponing pregnancy until later on in life runs counter to evolution. A woman begins her menstrual cycle right around her early teens which is an evolutionary signal that she can become pregnant. And there are complicated biological reasons behind it. In Pakistan and other countries, though it would be tough for you to conceive, pregnancy sometimes occurs beginning at the age of thirteen. Now I'm not recommending this—not at all—but just to suggest that, if a family with children is on your horizon, don't wait too long to tie the knot.

And now to technology-driven disappearing religion to the disappearing traditional family: I've already described how the attack on the existence of God is a huge factor leading to such disappearance. Covid has dramatically accelerated this trend because religious services and visits to the pastors and priest are much more difficult to arrange. The opposite occurred after 9/11 when the churches were filled to capacity. Men and women frequently have no one to talk to except on their computer which, like chastity, is a cold companion. Insecurity is everywhere—and growing.

Though not exactly related to religion, regarding security, there is a little appreciated but devastating blow that has been delivered by modern medical technology. In the not too distant past, doctors spent lots of time getting to know their patients, their families and other personal facts which played a huge role in helping patients adapt to the negative impact on their lives and feel more secure. Also, by such experience, doctors grew in wisdom and treatment know-how when patients' many signs and symptoms didn't fit into clear enough patterns to make a definitive diagnosis. Today, due to technology and management by business organizations, medicine has become impersonal, where the doctor is forced to spend about eight minutes with each patient in order to see enough patients to make money, which is the purpose of business. This is not an anti-business position but just a fact. If you don't make money you go out of business.

Getting back to religion: for reasons that truly puzzle and really disturb me, there is an almost universal absence of effective leaders in all walks of life including in the realm of religion. Religious leaders such as John Paul II and the Reverend Billy Graham are nowhere to be found. Without such leaders I fear, as said of old soldiers by General McArthur, religious leaders will simply fade away.

We have seen the effective elimination of traditional American values such as family, religion, neighborhood and healthy patriotism built up after generations of experience being rapidly replaced by technology-driven values. God is disappearing from our institutions, sex is now a free to express pleasure, the school names of Thomas Jefferson, Abraham Lincoln and George Washington are being cancelled, professional football players defy our national anthem and freedom of speech based on our first amendment may soon be a thing of the past.

What I forgot to mention is that humor, that wonderful medium that binds various subcultures and cultures, coupled frequently with the ability to laugh at oneself, has been suddenly cancelled. I've been fortunate to write for or appear on major media outlets but there is one distinguished newspaper that I've failed to crack. There was a depressing op-ed piece describing a new way to deliver humor without offending the sensitivities and sensibilities of ethnic and other minority groups. It was total rubbish. So I decided to write a letter to the editor describing what I thought was an acceptable "joke", remember that word?, that made people laugh. It goes as follows:

"A well-dressed man knocked at the door. The door was opened and there was a kid about 12 years old standing there with a can of beer in his hand, a lighted cigar in his mouth and a reversed baseball cap on his head. The man, somewhat taken aback, asked, "Is your daddy home?" The boy paused, removed the cigar from his mouth, smiled and answered, "What do you think?"

The editor said it was politically incorrect offending certain people. Whom it offended was not offered.

The nature and power of humor are little appreciated. Two of my favorite personalities are Benjamin Franklin and Winston Churchill. Any time I feel like I'm a bright guy, that feeling instantly disappears when I think of them. (Stephen Carlos, I'd strongly recommend that you read about these extraordinary great men.)

Julius Caesar's love affair with Cleopatra dramatically changed the course of history. Benjamin Franklin's many amorous affairs also dramatically changed history's course. This man was probably the horniest politician in America's history. He was a ladies' man and the women adored and chased him. Thomas Jefferson said that when Franklin was in a room with women, he could hardly control himself. Enviable man!

Because he was more than well-respected and popular, he was sent to England to convince King George to stop putting legal and economic pressure on the American colonies or they would revolt. He spent a number of years there having a good time with the ladies but failed in his mission. Thus came the American Revolution. Then he went to France and spent a few years trying to convince King Louis XVI to send troops to help George Washington defeat the British. With the help of his relationships with high level influential women, he managed to convince the King to send the troops, which immensely helped in the American victory.

Regarding these women, horny Benjamin found the French women much more attractive and more deliciously available than the British ladies. Now regarding humor, if told this story, most mature men and women would smile but today many would antagonistically label him as a womanizer, an accusation that lacks humor. Which takes me to my meeting with famous singer and personality, Frank Sinatra, and more about the current disappearance of the sex/humor connection.

When I was in college I was dating an attractive young lady whose father was a man with connections. Sinatra was performing at the now extinct 500 Club in Atlantic City and her father managed to get us good seats. During the performance, mature women, not teenagers or bobbysoxers, were emitting sounds of excitement and were actually on the verge of swooning. Her father arranged for us to meet Sinatra in his dressing room after the performance. At first glance, I knew why they called him "ol' blue eyes." He was sporting a clip-on bowtie, and I a hand-tied one. He asked me how I tied it, but we never got to a demonstration. I, being curious, asked him how he handled all those legions of adoring women in his life. He sat back on his chair and let out a mini-sigh and said, "Steve, if you're a star in show business, the women just keep coming on trying to get you in the bedroom. Yeah, it's a real compliment, but boy it can wear you out."

The reason why I bring this up is that the highly effective feminist movement driven by highly intelligent ones play down the fact that woman frequently chase, seduce and take advantage of men. In the past I've labeled them as "manizers." Feminist leaders, instead, daily employ the term "misogynist", men who hate women, and, "womanizers", men who are expert at seducing them. To add to their message, they view housewives with subtle disdain while glorifying career women.

Now it is not in the nature of men to form groups such as a "masculinist" movement to counter the feminist one, but let me tell you of my personal experiences. You both know that I traveled much of the world over the time span of half a century and frequently met thousands of men and women on a friendly basis, such as at dinner with good cocktails, good wine, good food and open, personal conversations. Though I know that they exist, particularly with increasing bitter divorce proceedings, I've never encountered a misogynist but have encountered a number of "misandrists" who are women who hate men. Now I'm quite sure you never heard of the word *misandry* which is the opposite of misogyny, and I want you to ask yourselves why this is so. It's quite a challenge for, despite the extensive literature on the social interaction between men and women, I never came across anyone asking that question, let alone using the word. The reason? Its omission is intentional.

In conclusion, the feminist movement, though certainly having important social messages, has been a potent anti-family force. Also, it's important to note that it is fundamentally *humorless*.

Before going to Winston Churchill let's take a look at what it's like to be a politician. It's no surprise they are almost always at the bottom of the popularity list in national polls whereas military personnel and medical doctors rate at the top. In perhaps the most famous Italian novel, *Il Gattopardo*, Don Fabrizio, the last of the great, historic *padrones* as Italy was entering modern times, was asked to become a national politician. He refused the offer. Why? He replied that he didn't have enough of the universal human characteristic of self-deception.

Politicians, in order to win an election, satisfy their constituents, raise money and win a re-election must necessarily make and break promises as well as support and vote for issues they fundamentally disagree with. Now with most men and women, this would be tough to do without the use of self-deception. Also, by repeatedly making such acts, it naturally becomes a habit requiring little or no soul searching and just becomes a routine part of the job.

Though you may be surprised, I am, in principle, not at all generally cynical about politics and politicians because this is the way our system has successfully worked in our country. I've personally known many politicians and they are generally good guys. I only met one high level female politician, Hillary Clinton, and must confess that I'm disappointed that she didn't have the opportunity of being our President. What I am cynical about, and so should you be, is how our system has recently and emotionally polarized into venomous warring factions. When, for example, our Senate votes one hundred percent along Democrat and Republican Party lines on much proposed legislation, you know that Senators in both parties at times don't believe in what they vote for, but in order to stay in power and receive party favors for their loyal behavior, they have, with the help of self-deception and, of course, also to maintain their power, little choice. And the situation is worsening today because of the many daily pressures placed upon them by self-interest, highly influential parties using cyberspace.

Now I'd like to point out what was hardly recognized as a newsworthy event but, to me, was a huge national catastrophe. In the past, Senators and House Representative Members of both parties generally stayed at their abodes in Washington, D.C. during the weekends. Many Democrats and Republicans frequently gathered together during the weekends either at their abodes or at restaurants to discuss past, present and future issues and legislation and developed a spirit of camaraderie and even friendship in attempting to do what was right for our country. Acceptable compromise was often agreed upon. Congress then decided to pay for members' expenses to return to their states on weekends to meet with their families and constituents. As a result, confidential and critical personal communication among its members soon dissipated. Currently, many members don't communicate at any time and a few even hate each other.

That's no way to run a business. To repeat, it's a national tragedy with no foreseeable remedy except maybe that which was demonstrated by Winston Churchill, who had a wonderful sense of humor.

In his later years, he continued to love politics and remained a member of the House of Commons which is similar to our Congress. As often occurs with great personalities who move mountains, he evoked much hate among members of the far-left Labour Party of the House who often subjected this old, historic giant to abuse. One day, as he was slowly leaving the chambers of the House, members of the far-left shouted out, "You're a rat," and, "You're leaving a sinking ship," and "Don't come back!"

Churchill suddenly paused, turned about to face the haters and graciously blew a number of kisses in their direction. This simple act of humor resulted in a burst of laughter from all members of the House, including the far-left ones. The lesson? Humor is a remedy that binds many different folks together and, as we have seen, is rapidly disappearing from the American culture. Hopefully, someone in Washington will soon bring it back to our politicians helping to bridge the current, destructive humorless chasm between Democrats and Republicans.

Let's switch subjects. There's a nameless force sweeping many segments of our culture that transgenderism is a small subset but highly symbolic representation of a rapidly trending movement which I call *Role Reversal*. Its scope is too much to cover in this book, however, it's critical to observe and wonder about. I see it all the time at my home by watching television which I sometimes do because Covid leaves me few options regarding my now limited daily activity.

Before I go on to *Role Reversal*, let me inform you about the nature of marketing which the public is not aware of. Marketing is the strategy to sell things and ideas ranging from dietary supplements to the pros and cons of presidential candidates. They can be simple ads or videos or podcasts, among others. You are inundated by marketing messages from dawn to bedtime effectively controlling your thoughts and desires that you and practically everyone else aren't aware of it. The Internet has made marketing, unlike chastity, a constant companion. In my career I've sat in on many marketing strategy sessions where plans are made on ways to sell a product or message. Now here's how it works.

There are two groups involved, marketing research that gathers the facts to be analyzed and the marketers who actually plan and execute or launch the marketing plan based on such facts. The research team surveys all the pertinent information available related to what is to be launched and frequently conducts their own surveys. It's very important here to note that they are actually measuring what's generally going on in the culture like the major political surveyors do in order to determine how to target the desired voting population. After they finalize a marketing plan, both groups conduct fascinating give-and-take sessions where selected members assume the role of consumers and how they would react to the marketing plan by asking and answering questions.

Once I came up with an idea regarding how to produce a high-dose, fat soluble, effervescent dietary supplement, which normally would take multiple pills to achieve. I spent lots of time on this product. I then managed to successfully have it reach the research-marketing team of one of our great American companies and sat in the session where it was evaluated as a potential candidate to market. As you are well aware, your grandpa can sometimes be overconfident, and I thought that the outcome would be a slam-dunk, but, unfortunately I was wrong and, as a result, lost a lot of time and money. But that's not the point. I was fascinated by how these bright men and women evaluated how the consumer would respond to the qualities and advantages of the product by analyzing the data and mindset of the buyer. Individuals played various creative roles asking critical questions.

But what also struck me like a lightning bolt, was the realization of how a small number of people can persuade millions to buy a product idea or belief. It was a frightening harbinger of what's going on today.

A while back men were beginning to be portrayed as dummies and their wives as wisdom-bearing ones taking charge and solving whatever problems they had. (Though I hate to admit it, there's some truth in that portrayal.) Soon after, weak-looking men appeared and continued to be portrayed taking care of babies, doing the laundry, washing the dishes, going shopping and other traditional female roles while the wives returned from work to check things out. The women are now portrayed as carpenters, mountain climbers and even Home plate baseball umpires calling strikes and balls. Erectile dysfunction is prominently displayed as the major problem in male-female sexual encounters while the common fact of females' lack of sexual desire is not at all portrayed. The only FDA approved drug to stimulate such women has been a flop. Also, blacks and women are everywhere in advertisements and video presentations where white males play a secondary role. Blue-eyed, blond males are nowhere to be found except in roles as the bad guys.

And here are some other revealing observations. Many Americans perceive the Japanese and Chinese physical appearances as typical Asian, not appreciating the varied physical attributes of other such Asians as Indonesian and Filipino, let alone India Indian. Increasingly, particularly with women, such Asians whose appearance is neither black, white nor typical Asian, but "of color", a now popular term, are increasingly appearing in advertisements.

What's interesting to observe is that Indians and Hispanics are not frequently portrayed. Maybe it's because Indians have been highly successful in our country and are not considered a minority. Regarding Hispanics, they have their own, distinct, vibrant culture with multiple Spanish speaking television stations. But for whatever reasons, the market researchers and marketers do not view them as general marketing opportunities for the public.

Remember, one of our best kept secrets is that advertising, or the process of convincing people to buy or buy into a product or message, oftentimes tells us what's going on in our culture simply because these creative marketing folks have first figured out what's going on and then target what they have to sell to these receptive audiences.

But there's another type of extremely influential, mind-controlling advertising which is not perceived to be advertising. Its marketing strategies are primarily delivered via television, newsprint and cyberspace. Unfortunately, it is oftentimes purposely misleading and even dishonest.

NEWS ALERT: SPEAKING OF ROLE REVERSAL! Though this will interrupt the continuum of my thoughts, this occurrence just happened, which is an anti-women, anti-mother and anti-family movement. Congressional House Speaker of San Francisco, Nancy Pelosi, is attempting to eliminate the traditional words of family and other relationships. She wants to eliminate the words father, mother, son, daughter, brother, sister, uncle, aunt, cousin, nephew, niece, husband, son-in-law, daughter-in-law from the language used in House deliberations. They would be replaced by gender neutral terms such as parent, child and sibling.

Author, Kimberly Ells, points out in a provocative piece, that Pelosi and her associates are supporting the ideology of the feminist socialist, Shulamith Firestone, who, during the '70s advocated the need to completely eliminate genital sex distinctions and that transsexuality should become the law of the land. Firestone, perhaps prophetically, predicted that when transsexuality becomes law, "The blood tie of the mother to the child would eventually disappear," followed by the "disappearance of motherhood." Ells points out that the current transgenderism movement may be the harbinger to the aforementioned. Transgendered boys and men with known superior physical capabilities can now compete in women's sports where, of course, they are usually the winners. In fact, newly elected President Biden has just signed a document making it okay.

Now, my grandchildren, pay particular attention to this. Transgenderism in sports would have been inconceivable not too long ago. It would have caused an uproar from all quarters and stopped cold in its tracks. Today, all is quiet. Mothers and fathers feel helpless, and there are no effective leaders to represent them. I want you to ask yourselves why this is happening and why there are few, if any effective leaders and why the absence of a cultural uproar? Stumped? Don't worry, for I'll tell you why. It's the combination of Role Reversal and the unleashing of the BGL!

Chapter 9

WHERE ARE WE HEADING?

As I said before, though I hate to tell you, we are at super-speed departing from the traditional cultural to the pervasive technological one, where people are increasingly willing to surrender their privacy and, therefore, freedom to the forces of technology. It's like being in a culture of *volunteered-slavery* where there will be a few controlling, marketing-type leaders and the rest, followers. Family, religion and freedom are rapidly fading away. And remember what I told you: When long-held valued institutions disappear, others will replace them. And what, you may ask, are behind these technology-driven forces?

Now your grandfather has a vision of why, how and what the future holds, and, my grandchildren, it's not the best of news. As I said before, I was hesitant to write this book because it deals with current reality. Others have also urged me not to write the book. The great physician, Joseph DiPalma, often repeated his mantra that, "The truth is brutal." So if you decide not to continue reading the book and turn to your controlling smartphones, I'll understand. If not, here we go!

You and all others soon will be almost totally controlled by the combination of two major forces: the six human characteristics and Internet Democracy.

What then is Democracy? Bottom line, it's a system where all eligible citizens have the right to participate to determine what a country can do including its government. Plato, founding father President James Madison and a host of other highly respected minds of different political philosophies consider that Democracy as a way to bring equality to all would lead to a catastrophic political system leading to chaos and cruel mob rule due to excessive freedom. Rulers will take advantage of the chaos and dramatically reduce freedom. The French Revolution is a clear example of unleashed Democracy in action. It was led by Robespierre, a very evil guy, where citizens were murdered, churches destroyed and the production of guillotines could not keep up with the demand to make headless citizens of those the rulers of the state wanted to eliminate such as priests, nuns, men, women and even their children, those with unacceptable ideas, the wealthy and those who were against the revolution, or whom government leaders simply did not like. You know: the thrill of killing. The executions and blood-shedding were everywhere.

In late 19th century Russia, nihilism, the freedom to ignore traditional values and replace it with new ones, was rampant. It's a kind of functional Democracy somewhat similar to our modern day relativism and cancel-culture. One of my favorite minds, Fyodor Dostoevsky, who had 15 epileptic seizures a week, observing this surge in freedom, wrote, "Boundless liberty leads to boundless tyranny" predicting the oncoming of tyrannical Soviet Union Communism leaders. Lenin, the leader of the Communism movement said something like freedom is so very precious that it should be limited to a precious few.

I had a personal friend who was the president of a large corporation and who, as child, lived in an Eastern European country dominated by the Russian Communists. The Russian leaders in his country were granted total control over his people, including his family. I won't go into the brutal details but these leaders granted selected favors to the people by employing bribery, extortion, paying off informers, bargaining for sexual favors and even taking over the homes of some without recompense. They were a cruel lot. He and his family, by the use of bribery, managed to escape the country and come to what he called his "beloved America."

Now don't forget these two lessons! The first one: One of the best kept and intentionally suppressed lessons of history is that freedom and equality are mortal enemies. The more equality, the less there is of freedom—and, vice versa. The second one: Democracy is, by far, the most effective political system to permit the full expression of the six human characteristics: self-interest, self-deception or rationalization, recognition, power-money, competition and altruism. And as we have seen, the ultimate result of this combination is evil!

Getting back to Democracy and evil, our Founding Fathers were well aware of this inextricable connection and figured out a way of granting sufficient freedom to its citizens to effectively suppress evil and also would encourage them to become productive and thrive. Much of their thinking was influenced by the French philosopher, Montesquieu, who influenced the Constitution's provision of three national government branches, the executive, legislative and judicial. By doing so, there would be checks and balances placed on each branch that seeks too much power by placing restrictions on the expression of the six human characteristics. It worked beautifully, but now, my grandchildren, our Constitution is being seriously challenged.

Before proceeding, it's critical to note that currently you are exposed to the terms the Left and Right as distinct political entities. There are other terms such as Kingdoms, Communism, Socialism, Capitalism, and other "oms" and "isms" in understandable attempts to define the nature of governments particularly because they invariably change and are in transition over time. But the way to judge the nature of government, be it Left or Right or whatever, is not by its label but by considering to what degree the individual has freedom which takes us to our current technology-driven, destabilizing infatuation with Socialism. As of now we are, step by inexorable step instead of revolutionary ones, heading toward the Left, be it what is called Socialism or whatever. Don't be surprised if, depending on how the government will control you and everybody else except those, of course, who govern, the government will be labeled as Right. Why? Because it becomes obvious, as with a dictator, instead of subtlety tyrannical. What's going on now?

Now listen to your grandfather regarding the reasons why things are going out of control in our country. *It's the synergistic combination of Democracy and the Internet!* Remember that I told you that Democracy is the full expression of the six human characteristics where everyone has something to say, and the net effect of the interactions of the six is evil. Today, the Internet within just a few decades, has become a Universal Democracy where nearly everyone has the ability to express their thoughts and opinions. And, *pari passu*, hate, the potent and highly infectious destabilizing expression of evil, is increasingly dominating cyberspace and much of our daily lives. This venom is permeating everything from personal relationships to local communities to the highest levels of our national government. And, as day follows night, this excessive freedom of expression will not endure and will be replaced by some other controlling system where there will be a vast reduction of such freedom and manipulation of our cultural values and behavior.

MY TAKE ON THE INTERNET DEMOCRACY

Let's now take a look at the six characteristics with respect to former President Trump, race, gender and equity movements which are sweeping the landscape of our country by starting out with Mr. Trump.

If I say anything about Trump that's positive, one-half of our country will immediately turn off, refusing to consider my reasoning. If I say something negative, the other half will do likewise. "Why is this?" you may ask. Believe it or not, your grandfather can sometimes be humble and admit I simply don't know. But I do have a theory. It may have, in part, something to do with the evolution of the Emoji brain's interpretations of past icon experiences as positive or negative and somehow connecting the Trump icon to such experiences.

Let's start out with the Left which is our current major cultural force, but it, to repeat, may eventually turn to the Right. The Left is currently dominated by the Democratic Party while the Right is currently weakly represented by the Republican Party. The Left tenaciously views Mr. Trump with absolute hate. I review multiple types of media outlets daily where, coupled with this hate, and though I "hate" to say this, are obvious outright lies and manipulation of facts, which is a subtle form of masking lies. My personal opinion is that many of these media men and women, because of the high level of emotional hate, are captives of self-deception, actually believing that they are reporting the truth and supporting a worthy cause. After all, the end justifies the means. So what's new? The Right or conservative media, a much smaller cultural force, do the same but to a much, much lesser degree. It seems that one of its major roles is to play defense by refuting the manipulative messages of the Left.

Here's something by the Left that should scare you. One prominent member of the Democratic Party proposed that we must re-educate the 74 million citizens who voted for Mr. Trump. Farfetched? Maybe not.

Before going on here is a revealing thought experiment like Schrodinger's Cat that I conducted regarding Mr. Trump. I contacted a number of friends and colleagues of both the Left and Right and in-between by email, all good people, and asked the following questions, "Given the fact that Trump did a reasonable job regarding the economy and made attempts to reduce foreign wars, both of which all Americans desire, why do a large percentage of Americans hate him while the others do not? To be sure his personality is quite rough and gruff and many attribute it to that cause. But let's assume that you had an extremely surgically difficult brain tumor to extract and that one of the world's superb brain surgeons would be available to operate on you, but his personality was quite similar to Mr. Trump's. In addition, in the past he was charged for a wife-beating episode. For the aforementioned two reasons, would you turn him down and choose a much lesser talented neurosurgeon to operate on you? What is your answer?"

Well, would you believe, I didn't receive a single well-reasoned response. All, with emotions running high, attacked the others with vituperative barbs. The haters rejected the neurosurgeon analogy. One of the haters then, in a classic case of self-deception, cited the great theologian, Aquinas, who wrote that all analogies are faulty. I responded by disagreeing pointing out that the Emoji brain would clearly accept it. The non-haters, of course, welcomed and embraced the analogy. Incredibly, none rationally answered the fundamental question regarding why people either hate or do not hate Mr. Trump.

Olivia and Stephen Carlos think about this, for these different mentalities say a lot about human nature and how people both think and feel.

And this is very critical to understand: the amount and degree of hatred of Mr. Trump would never have occurred without the unique biased view of the Internet Democracy.

Before we go on, have you ever asked yourself, "What is the Internet? What are its functions and who controls them?"

Before we address these questions, I'd like to once more stress the types of news which most attract the public. It's the bad, the controversial and the sensational! Reporting on the stabbings and killings on Manhattan subways attract far more attention than news reporting a peaceful subterranean day. What would attract more attention in the following scenario: If Presidents Biden and Trump played golf together and they posted their scores at the 18th hole, or if they had a fist-fight afterwards in the 19th hole or clubhouse where Trump lost one of his front teeth and Biden suffered a broken nose?

Now here's a revealing example that really disturbs me regarding the timid, unforgiveable silence of those who should not be. It deals with the Catholic Church which has been continually besieged with sexual scandals that all media outlets have understandably trumpeted for it's the lethal combination of the bad and evil, the controversial and the sensational news. This event plus other forces of technology are leading to an exodus of its flock. And what has the Church done to respond to this crisis? It has retreated instead of boldly confronting it. And, "What," you may ask, "would your grandfather do?"

One of the best kept secrets regards the enormity of the good that the Church does throughout much of the world. In the United States it operates 600 church-sponsored hospitals, 1,400 long-term facilities and 7,500 schools for 2.3 million students. There are about 18,000 churches and 2,500 missions to attend to its flock. That's a lot of good that even the vast majority of Catholics don't know about. Are you wondering why?

If I were the Pope, I'd hire a public relations firm with a long-term agreement to come up with a strategy to promote this altruistic mission, and even add the message that individuals, families and institutions are all a mixture of the good and bad which essential wisdom is completely absent today where the bad dominates. The public relations firm should somehow market the core message of Jesus, who said to the crowd that was about to stone an adulterer to death, "He who is without sin let him cast the first stone."

Another memory just jumped to mind. A while back before you were born, I had lunch with the Pope's confessor and a very high member of the Jesuit Order at a small restaurant just off the Via Veneto in Rome. We covered a few subjects, one of which was the oncoming of the world-wide web and the need for the Church to heavily employ it. Of course, the Church never caught on and continues to pay the price.

Olivia and Stephen Carlos, you may wonder why I spent so much time on the Church. It's one of my few pet peeves regarding the woeful general lack of leaders in many sectors, and now that I've got it out of my system, let's return to the *Internet Democracy*.

Let's divide it into the following categories: Information and Communication in General, Obvious Hysterical Propaganda, Subtle Unopposed Propaganda with an Hysterical Component and Surveillance.

Information and Communication in General are the most frequently used and somewhat understood accepted functions, but not so with the other three, which takes us to an underappreciated power of the Internet: its capacity to cause mob or mass hysteria, hysteria being defined as a dynamic irrational, psychosocial emotional response related to an event or other issues. Historically, they have been small, limited happenings such as in the Salem Witch Hunt and the tarantella dance and occasionally large ones such as in the French Revolution and Nazi Germany. The events were usually triggered orally or by local and national media outlets triggering national hysteria. Hate, fear, anxiety, panic and insecurity are the inevitable outcomes.

In conclusion, you and all others, except the rulers, of course, will be within the near future controlled by the state or government. Now follow this: I've been describing what's going on in the United States but I see it happening, in one way or another, worldwide. It has to do with potential weapons of warfare.

Let's say there are generally four types of weapons: regular, nuclear, cyberspace and biological. And, one of our best kept secrets, with high level exceptions, all are dramatically expanding in sophistication and lethality including means of delivery. During the Vietnam War, I was stationed at WRAIR, the Walter Reed Army Institute, and learned that the Pentagon was instrumental in developing cyberspace technology or the Internet, the primary purpose of which was to aid in military communications, particularly in difficult times. The worldwide Internet was then non-existent. (By the way, you should be proud that your grandfather was an Army captain.)

One day I had lunch at the Officers Club with one of our top cyberspace experts. Though the impact of what he said did not then strike me, he stated that all computer systems could be hacked and that some other non-hackable systems apart from the Internet must be developed in order to maintain absolute secrecy. His prediction, unfortunately, seems to be true. We are now almost totally dependent on cyberspace technology. All systems from individual, corporate and military ones are being hacked daily by the millions and our anti-hack systems are in a losing race unable to stop them. FYI, I haven't yet come cross one media coverage of our hackable Internet threat. I'd like you to pause and ask yourselves why, because I don't have an answer.

What really worries me about cyberspace is it doesn't require a large technological savvy government or organization to penetrate and control it, or any other system but only a few brilliant, creative guys. I say "guys" because, like warfare in general, it's primarily a man thing. For example, some entity can penetrate our military system not only by shutting it down but by turning it against itself. They can, as a middle- man in a foreign country, guide one of our nuclear missiles on a Russian city and the Russians, of course, will retaliate against the United States with one or more nuclear weapons sparking a vastly destructive nuclear war.

Also, at WRAIR I collaborated with my good friend and scientist, Major James Vick, who also worked with the scientists at Edgewood Arsenal, the institution responsible for evaluating toxins, viruses and bacteria including their potential as weapons of biological warfare.

One day the Major and I met with an expert on historic bacterial and viral plagues such as the Black Death and the Spanish Flu. It then dawned on me that we currently had at least potential antibiotics or the capacity to produce new ones to treat bacterial pandemics and plagues but few antiviral drugs to treat the viral ones. We only had a couple of vaccines, which took years and lots of know-how to produce, and only a couple of pharmaceutical companies had such capacities.

Now let's take a jump ahead to Covid, which as I said scares the shit out of me for reasons other than its existence. Both of you and practically all others believe that vaccines are the answer to the Covid pandemic and after that all will be well. Not so. Not even close! We now have breakthrough genetic technologies such as CRISPR and gain-in-function where the genetics of a single harmless virus, let alone a lethal one such as Covid, can be "easily" and inexpensively made to be virulent or much more virulent. A big operation is not needed to conduct this experiment. A solitary, well-funded madman scientist in his private laboratory can secretly bioengineer one or more viruses, and it is impossible to detect these guys. Now multiply these scientists by the thousands, many of whom are sponsored by governments both large and small, and the probability of discovering and globally spreading more viruses which are as lethal or more lethal than the Spanish flu is a reality to be confronted. Before I forget, viruses in general such as Covid can naturally mutate becoming resistant to vaccines. Not only that, but even with our wonderful new technology, spurred on by Operation Warp Speed, we cannot possibly develop vaccines for each new virus. Even if one is discovered it takes multi-thousands of volunteers to clinically test the effectiveness of each individual one.

Not so with drugs such as penicillin and insulin where it would take a small number of patients in a very brief period of time to demonstrate their effectiveness: perhaps a couple of dozen with insulin in diabetic coma and the same number with penicillin in patients with bacterial lobar pneumonia. Physician and former FDA Commissioner and someone to listen to, Scott Gottlieb, wrote that there are hundreds of anti-Covid drugs in the pipeline which is good news. But that's just a single virus. Will these targeted drugs be effective against all variants and other viruses? No, they won't, but it would be a huge step forward to discover other effective ones.

As a proposed forward strategy I wrote, "The solution is to expeditiously –speed is critical!–create a coalition of government, pharmaceutical, bioengineering and private entrepreneurial groups not to deal with the discovery of vaccines or treatments such as pharmaceuticals and biologicals, but focus on the basic core mechanisms of viral and bacterial behavior which is a formidable task and critical challenge which is not doable by a single pharmaceutical or other research organizations. After all, these organisms have, by constant adaptation under the most adverse environmental conditions, survived over billions of years. And, by doing so, they have evolved multiple mechanisms for survival. For example, how do bacteria protect their walls and how do viruses replicate themselves?

"Once these basic mechanisms are discovered, then the companies or institutions that have the capacity and know-how on ways to conduct research on vaccines and treatment therapies can readily employ these discoveries to build upon, which will substantially increase the probability of success. Frankly speaking, as little as twenty years ago, I would not, even if the coalition were formed, be optimistic regarding a near-term success, but the recent explosion of technology from artificial intelligence to bioengineering are solid grounds for optimism."

In the past, my physician colleague and then Senate Majority Leader, Bill Frist, warned that viral and bacterial epidemics are on their way and we are defenseless against them. And he recently repeated his warning at a Senate Hearing. His warnings and the undisputed fact that treatment drugs or biologicals (which are natural drugs) are the way to go, has been ignored by the medical experts, government authorities and investigative media. Pause again and ask yourselves why. I have and don't have an answer to this huge cultural blind spot. In the past, the famous Prussian general, Carl von Clausewitz, wrote, "War is an act of force to compel our enemy to do our will." And the threat of biological warfare is such an act.

FYI, you can read more about my thoughts on this subject on my website for The Foundation for Innovation in Medicine, which I founded way before you were born in 1976, at www.fimdefelice.org.

And though not nearly as capable of delivery as the aforementioned weapons of warfare, conventional warfare weapons are exploding. For example, we have 12 nuclear submarines stationed throughout the world carrying nuclear warheads that can destroy a city or more. Their locations are, of course, supposedly a secret. The Russians are now developing underwater drones with the capacity to detect and destroy such submarines. Suppose they do it? What do you think would happen? Take a pause here and think about it.

There are two classic books regarding the future of the world governments written by two starkly different personalities, Aldous Huxley and George Orwell, which probably reflected their diverse futuristic visions. Huxley's book, *Brave New World*, describes a society where people were contented to be controlled and dominated. One method employed by the rulers was to give all the people "soma" which was, more or less, a happy pill bringing about broad-based contentment. In Orwell's book, *1984,* the rulers employ heavy propaganda, a method of brainwashing, combined with sometimes brutal, forceful tools. No soma to be found in Orwell country!

It's interesting to note that Hitler effectively employed the combination of all three—propaganda, brutal force and drugs. He fed his soldiers crystal meth which gave them boundless energy without the need of sleep for long periods of time which also created a mindset of unparalleled cruelty which you probably know all about. You should read about the Blitzkrieg and how the German Army at incredible speed conquered a large swath of Europe. In addition, crystal meth was freely available like aspirin in a pharmacy to its citizens. Hitler, himself, took crystal meth and opioids which I believe was, in a strange way, a godsend. The formidable German military-scientific complex was a magnificent machine far superior than any existing one. The atom bomb, rockets, jet planes and biological warfare capability were well on their way to becoming developed and operational. If Hitler would have waited until then, he might have conquered the world. But I believe his drug-taking made him extremely impatient and by feeding his megalomania robbed him of his judgement.

During World War II, the Japanese military were also big takers of crystal meth. The Kamikaze suicide pilots took large doses intravenously before they crashed into American and other ships. The Japanese bonsai suicide charging troops took the oral dose before leaving planet earth.

It's interesting to note that these two powerful war powers became spectacular economic successes after their defeat. Think about what's behind this connection. What do you think?

As you know, your grandfather has lots of experience in the evaluation and clinical testing of pharmaceutical drugs, evaluating their effectiveness and safety. Early on I learned that the brain's neurotransmitters are highly receptive to all kinds of substances, both natural and synthetic. I would bet that in the future soma and other types of pleasurable drugs will dominate the world's landscape, leading to almost absolute control by its leaders. And, with exploding modern technology, they will not be too difficult to discover and produce.

In conclusion, given the nature of those humans who seek power, the use of regular, nuclear, cyberspace and biological weapons will inevitably go out of control. It can be a person or some type of entity such as an ambitious government. And, the entire world might surrender to whatever it is.

There are all types of possibilities one of which I saw in the movies when I was a kid and later on television. It was about a crazy guy hovering over the earth in a spacecraft loaded with a deadly weapon that could destroy much of mankind. He wants the earth to surrender to his power or an enormous amount of ransom money. Frankly speaking, I thought he was kind of a dumb guy for asking for the money for where would he be able to spend it? It's a complicated scenario, and I'll leave it at that!

Though there are a number of ways in which this world control can be obtained, I think that the easiest and least expensive way, particularly for a small group headed by a megalomaniac, can be achieved by genetic bioengineering of an extremely lethal virus or bacterium. By the way, the world is full of such guys, and they may be in your own neighborhood. Just ask your father, who's a great reader of people. Your mother is too full of love to accept the existence of such evil creatures.

Here is what he'll do. After he creates this virulent microorganism, he would also discover an antidote, probably a drug, and produce both in massive quantities to handle large populations. Then he would place the viruses or bacteria in drones and guide them to a number of the world's major capitols, release the microorganism and most of their citizens would agonizingly suffer and die. As an aside, do you know there are about a million drones in our country which can be targeted to any site such as the Pentagon and Wall Street? Something to think about, isn't it?

Let's say, the megalomaniac will then make the offer, "Surrender to me or much of the world will die. I also have the antidote to stop the spread." And, of course, the world would surrender. But that wouldn't be the final step. How then would the megalomaniac rule the world?– which you never see in the movies.

Let's take an historic look at how tyrants who had complete control over their people ruled. Many are generally fundamentally cruel and sadistic beyond human comprehension, and so will be the megalomaniac. The one that makes the blood curdle the most was the Romanian tyrant, Vlad the Impaler, from Dracula's land of Transylvania. He inserted a smooth pole into the human rectum or vagina and pushed it through the body until it exited near the neck or the mouth. It was like a skewered shish kabob. He made sure the pole wasn't sharp, for that would immediately kill the victim, and he wanted to make them live a day or so in order for him to enjoy the show. It's said that he skewered about 20,000 souls and created a mini forest composed of many of them. Just imagine what that would look like!

But let's jump to the 20th century to Stalin of Russia, Hitler of Germany, Mao Zedong of China, Tojo of Japan and Pol Pot of Cambodia. All were men of incomprehensible cruelty and perversion, who had multi- millions of citizens, tortured, murdered and forced to live under predictable fatal conditions. Babies were not even spared; in fact, the henchmen of these tyrants expressed joy in killing the babies using different perverted ways. Such is the thrill of having and exercising absolute power such as ripping the fetuses from the wombs of their mothers.

During the '70s, I had the privilege of having permission to enter the United Nations in Manhattan where I met many high level international diplomats and ambassadors. One day, while having lunch with a foreign representative, he told me of a current tyrant who, while sitting in a chair having a drink and smoking a cigar, had men brought before him and had them totally castrated in order to have his BGL thrill, if you know what I mean.

It's not the purpose of this book to delve into the details of the evil of tyrants but just to demonstrate what can happen when one continues to surrender one's freedom.

MORE ON THE INTERNET DEMOCRACY

Before we go on, let's once more examine the details of Internet dynamics. To repeat, have you ever asked yourselves, "What is the Internet and what are its functions and who controls them?" And don't forget it's an Internet Democracy where, as you shall see, the interplay all of six human characteristics are at play and evil manifested in hate or cruelty sadly is the winner!

To repeat, the Internet can be divided into five parts: Information, Communication, Obvious Hysterical Propaganda, Subtle Unopposed Propaganda with an Hysterical Component, and Surveillance. As I said before, most are aware of the first two parts but not so with the last three which I'll now address.

Obvious Hysterical Propaganda: Have you ever seen an hysterical, excitable person whose emotions go way out of control oftentimes leading to powerful negative thoughts and behavior? If not, check out a few movies on your computer for it's a common event in the entertainment sector. Hysterical moments have no limitations on cruel expressions.

The Internet has changed all that. It's constant 24/7 and almost everywhere creating, I fear, permanent expanding moments of out-of-control national hysteria and hate. The Internet Democracy fueled by the Left create the hysterical hatred for Mr. Trump, but demeaned his innocent wife who suffered cruel barbs. Ladies' magazines, fearful of losing much of their readers, never, despite her beauty and ability to speak a number of languages, placed her on their covers while placing a previous president's wife on a number of them. The recent death of the famous conservative radio host giant, Rush Limbaugh, has met with a torrent of Internet-fueled hysterical hatred actually rejoicing over his death simply because of his political philosophy and ability to professionally critique the Left. Now think of this. When the Supreme Court Justice and understandably heroine of the Left and opponent of the Right, Ruth Bader Ginsburg, passed away shortly before Limbaugh, the Right was silent which, to repeat, reflects revealing mental-emotional differences between the two groups. Why do you think this is so?, for it says a lot. As I said before, could it be that it's due to the evolutionary process dividing the human brain into two separate groups? How would you describe them?

Speaking of evolution and the future, the forefinger, because of clicking, the thumb, because of texting, and the rear-end, because of sitting all day in front of computers, will all substantially grow in size!

The Obvious Hysterical Propaganda phenomenon is a clear attempt to suppress and control by suppressing the freedom of expression and action by others by creating waves of fear and hate.

Regarding too much Left leading to too much Right, I'll address later on when I'll mention Napoleon. Speaking about the Frenchman, Napoleon, if he were born a few weeks earlier, he would have been an Italian! The French took over the then Italian Corsica a few weeks before his birth.

Subtle Unopposed Propaganda with an Hysterical Component: Olivia and Stephen Carlos, pay particular attention to this category, for this is wherein lies the major force and interplay of our current Internet Democracy. It includes multiple categories such as diversity, racism gender expression, woke, cancel culture, white supremacy and others. All are forces which, by the way, are overlapping energetically supporting increased government powers and decreased human freedom. *Now keep this in mind. They are all in some way attempts to increase equity by increasing government power. Equity is a new term used by the Left to replace the term equality. Bottom line, equity means government forcing equality by laws, regulations and rules. It's fundamentally a quota system in disguise.* When these forces are combined they are a formidable weapon to increase government power. So let's take a look at the dynamics of this emerging power.

Regarding subtle propaganda, remember when I pointed out that governments, particularly aggressive and revolutionary ones, effectively employ subtle mind-controlling messages where the truth is intentionally distorted and manipulated but the people take them as truth. I say that the current Internet Democracy forces are largely unopposed because there is little effective opposition to them. Succinctly put, they are winning. Attempts at propaganda in the past were amateurish compared to the Pied Piper of the 24/7 Internet Democracy.

Regarding the Hysterical component, it has to do with the distortion of altruism, one of the characteristics of the six, which is generally considered a beautiful and charitable quality of the human mind. Remember, it's analogous to the Bible's Golden rule, "Do unto others as you would have them do unto you."

Now here's how the very savvy, and may I say oftentimes sincere and understandably thrilled by their growing power, men and women of relatively small numbers plan and launch their strategies to influence and control the thoughts, feelings and actions of the large public. Each separate force aided by the persistent 24/7 Internet bombardment, transmits messages based on emotion subtly and *carefully avoiding the use of reason.* Emotion is the best way to strike at the hearts of Americans, a country that historically generally favors the underdog, where they, like a flame put to hay, respond with an urgent call to action to do the apparent good. The trick, once more, is to avoid rational discussion. Unfortunately, there is an integral hysterical component to this cultural emotional response, as witnessed by all kinds of destructive demonstrations and the pervasive spread of intense irrational hate that divides Americans. And don't forget that the right amount of hate is a driving force that brings about dramatic change bringing power to the Left culture-changers. But again, here's my mantra and concern: If the Left goes too far and the people tire of it, which is not farfetched, the Right will take its place.

Surveillance: Now my grandchildren, we've already made the obvious observation that humans love technology and are willing to sacrifice their privacy including where and how many times they went to the lavatory the day before yesterday and what happened there let alone in the bedroom.

Let's now take a look two examples of the major forces with an hysterical component—racism and transgenderism. When trying to analyze an objective overview or big picture of certain social phenomena key questions must be asked. Let's ask them regarding racism and the Black population.

- What is the definition of racism in general?
- What is the evidence that it "currently" exists for the Black population?
- If so, what are the dynamics behind it?
- What, therefore, is the general solution?

Now, my dear grandchildren, to my knowledge these questions have never been asked regarding the Black population. If they have been published somewhere, they are intentionally ignored. I've written about it, and it has also been ignored. The belief that racism exists is now rapidly sweeping the nation primarily based on emotional marketing with an hysterical anti-white supremacist component largely focused on white males. President Biden has proclaimed that white supremacy permeates all levels of government and promises to do something about it. There is little doubt that his objective is now leading to substantial social division and hate.

Critical Race Theory is another rapidly growing anti-white movement being part of the woke and cancel culture ones even supported by some well-meaning men and women. Its basic premise is that our legal system and other institutions are structured to suppress non-whites, the assumption being the latter are equal. Another assumption that its proponents avoid is that though there are distinctive physical differences among peoples, there are no mental ones. This assumption is rarely discussed and you should think about why this is so.

Now I don't want to address the pros and cons of the Critical Race Theory, but the vast majority of its supporters are clearly emotionally begging the question which means making an assumption before examining the facts. For example, one of the most widely suppressed white groups in our Western culture are the Jews. Though some fact-checking may not exactly support the numbers, 20 percent of Nobel Prize winners are Jews. The Jews comprise 2 percent of the United States' population, yet 50 percent of our billionaires. Much of the media from television to Hollywood is managed by Jews. This, my grandchildren, is something to consider.

Before I go on, you are a cultural mixture of Italian and Hispanic Mexican. Up until recently, Italians were not considered to be white and were generally looked down upon. I checked my notes and found that a court decision generally banning hanging as a type of national execution applied to all people except Blacks and Italians. During my youth, I experienced lots of anti-Italian moments which, paradoxically, like lightning striking Frankenstein, made me stronger. Interestingly enough, not too long ago, at a dinner gathering celebrating the Scottish poet Robert Burns, Patricia Park, who is of Scottish ancestry, was warned by a Scottish woman about the dangers of Italian men while I was sitting at the same table within earshot. In a sense, I took that as a compliment, if you know what I mean!

Now this is something to think about and also to take advantage of. As I said before, there's a budding growing movement to equate "people of color' with the Black population offering the same advantages to this group. If you think about it, this term includes everyone except whites. To also share in these new rights I would suggest to label yourselves as such people in order to take the increasing advantages granted to them. It's too late for your grandfather for it is written in Ecclesiastes of the Old Testament that, "For everything there is a season." And, Olivia and Stephen Carlos, my season is just about over.

Now to the complexity of transgenderism: Remember when I mentioned the Brain Genital Law or BGL proposing that all sexual behavior is natural because the roots of its origins and expressions are naturally rooted in the brain. This unequivocally holds true with transgenderism. But also remember the caveat: there are many dark sides to the freedom of sexual as well as other types of behavioral expression, and the current transgender movement has its dark side one being to substantially increase government control over the personal behavior of Americans. And, as I mentioned before, the leader of this movement is President Biden fulfilling a promise made to the Left before he was elected president. He has proposed the Equality Act which law, in part, would encourage the actual persecution of those who oppose transgenderism and its freedom. Thus men who transgender into women would have the same rights as women such as in their dressing rooms, bathrooms, women's dormitories, on their sports teams and in the military. Religious churches would lose their rights and face persecution in their charities and adoption agencies if they maintain their beliefs and policies to treat men and women as naturally biologically different. It's interesting to note that almost the entire media coverage deals, in laudatory language, with transgendered men but, for puzzling reasons, transgendered women are being ignored. Why do you think this is so? Also, if you think about it, the Equality Act is, in part, an anti-women one yet feminists groups have remained strangely silent. Why do you think this also is so?

You'd be surprised to know there is very little reliable, quantifiable human data regarding the biological and psychological nature of this sexual phenomenon making it extremely difficult to determine ways to manage it particularly when dealing with the very young and making sure they are not inexcusably damaged. Also, aggressive, emotion-driven influential parties, and they are emotional, are pushing many confused children and adults to change sexes despite not knowing such outcomes. And without doubt much unreportable harm has already occurred and more is on its way. Who are these parties and what makes them authorities on sexual changes? FYI, they do not exist!

Now here's something that both infuriates and depresses me regarding transgenderism. It's how both parents and physicians are changing the sexes of innocent children, including young teenagers, which is oftentimes irreversible, without, to repeat, the slightest idea of how it will affect their lives both in the near and long-term, particularly on their minds and quest for happiness. *This is a clear case of human experimentation.* In medicine, if a potential new therapy such as a Covid vaccine or antibiotic is to be appropriately administered to children in medical practice, it must first be tested in a clinical study in order to determine whether it is both effective and reasonably safe. Such clinical studies should be obligatory in transgender transformation procedures that usually combine surgery with drug therapy. And, unlike the clinical testing of many new therapies, however, these studies would unquestionably be difficult to design, let alone carried out. Without doubt, the attempts at human experimentation in children and young teenagers should be heavily regulated in order to protect them.

Regarding adults, they should be free to do what they want though, as with children, the nature of their future is both unknown and complicated. I recently met a woman whose lady friend's nineteen-year-old son transgendered into a female but decided to retain his penis. When asked the reason behind his decision, he wanted to make absolutely sure that he would not lose his capacity to achieve an orgasm. The woman then wondered that he was about to enter a co-ed college, and what would be the rules if he wanted to stay at a woman's dormitory and, let's say, take a shower and do other things which exposed his organ. Complicated, isn't it?

There is little doubt that this irresponsible behavior of parents and physicians is largely due to two factors: the deregulation of the BGL where much sexual behavior is now condoned and combined with the hysteria of the Internet Democracy.

Big hate-provoking battles on the implementation of transgender policies are on their way particularly in the domain of religion. Court battles are on their way.

Olivia and Stephen Carlos, as I pointed out, we are in the rapidly advancing interim phase leading from the traditional world to that of the technological one. We have seen that the nature of the interim phase is saturated with intense hate both dividing and weakening our culture. Clearly stated, we are in a country that is spiraling out of control.

And, remember, at this moment, it is the Left that is the driving force of such change led by the universities, big business, corporations, Hollywood, the media, the government and Big Tech, the Internet giants. Big Tech principally includes the Internet giants of Apple, Google, Twitter,

Amazon and Facebook, who directly or indirectly control the information flow to the public. It's revealing to note that the employees of Big Tech supported presidential candidate Hillary Clinton, a symbol of the Left, 60-1 against President Trump. And Big Tech will play a huge role in the oncoming of the technological world. And, my grandchildren, Big Tech is largely unregulated. And, therefore, so are its employees who have critical information about all.

Tempting, isn't it, when you think about human nature including you and me? What would you do with that kind of power if you had a driving political philosophy as is common today?

Anyway, I kind of saw this happening a few decades ago, and don't forget this: it's largely about the equity-equality movement and the crusades by a media-wise minority to rob people of their freedom by increased government control. To repeat, equality and freedom are sworn enemies and there is an absence of national leaders to effectively stem the tide of loss of freedom except for the possibility of the Supreme Court which will be interesting to watch. There's little doubt that in the coming years a number of key cases, particularly regarding the Constitution, will be brought before the Court. Its members are under lots of pressure augmented by the Democrat party's mission to increase its judges who philosophically favor more government control citing the Living Constitution as a rationale which basically means that the principles of this document can be changed depending on the times an which also means an absence of durable and reliable standards. These new principles will be highly influenced by the Internet Democracy of which you both are captive members. And, don't be surprised that future Supreme Court decisions will be ignored which will cause an hysterical national battle over our Constitution

And now, to Napoleon and the Italian word, "*basta.*" As of this writing, there is an increasing awareness by men and women of all stripes that things are going out of control, and they are becoming fed up with the pervasive chaos enveloping our nation. *Basta* is a strong expression of "Enough"! And, I believe, a *Basta* moment is in the air.

Now remember what I told you that when there is change something must replace it. After the Left French Revolution the people had enough, *basta,* and turned to the Right represented by Napoleon. Now it is not farfetched to conceive of a charismatic president who has loyal support of the military to take over and become some type of dictatorship where our Constitution will be no more.

So, my grandchildren, what advice have I to give to you regarding how to adapt to your freedom-less future? So here goes.

Socialism: The in-word now is Socialism where the Left is employing it to deceive the public. Interestingly enough, young folks are very attracted to and largely controlled by the misrepresentation of the term. But as I said before, you can only judge a government not by its title but by the degree to which it controls you. And, Socialism or not, you are being increasingly controlled. And, historically Socialism is a logical step to Communism. And never forget this: *government is people* and not some abstract structure. As I mentioned before, in Sweden the government has been considering having a government employee having the responsibility to monitor the entire family life. Think about someone you really don't like in your neighborhood or elsewhere who will have control over you and your family. This is not a farfetched thought-experiment but somehow, some way, I fear that something similar is on its way.

Chapter 10

THE REVEALING LESSONS
OF CARNITINE

Let's switch gears and talk about the lessons of carnitine regarding why we have so much preventable disease and suffering today. Though carnitine has played a major role in my life, you probably aren't even aware of its existence. I bring it up because it helped me pursue a purpose in life, and I urge you to seek and find your purpose and your "carnitine" to help make it happen. It's too complicated and long a story to cover here so I'll only mention some critical points. (If you're interested there's a book written about my fascinating journey with it. *A Maverick's Odyssey, One Doctor's Quest to Conquer Disease* by Michael Mannion. Why not buy it?–for your grandfather could use the money!)

Do you remember my night with my comatose grandmother and my failed attempted bargain with God, one consequence being the birth of my hatred of disease? Well, it never left me. When I was a third-year medical student I decided that I couldn't accept another penny from my father so–now listen to this–I got a job in charge of an accident ward now known as an emergency room with just one aide to help me out. I treated lots of emergencies from gunshot wounds to the delivery of babies, which, in case you don't know it, is an emergency! I worked every other night and every other weekend for two years, and what an experience it was. One eye-opening lesson learned was my observation of the importance of natural substances such as penicillin and insulin for the treatment of disease.

After graduation from Jefferson Medical School, I trained there as an endocrinologist and then as a clinical pharmacologist at St. Vincent's Medical Center in New York, the latter being the specialty on how to study drugs in people instead of animals. (Before I forget, your father was born at St. Vincent's while I was there.) I had my own private clinical research facility in Connecticut State Prison where I evaluated the safety and effectiveness of new drugs administered for the first time in prison volunteers with promising drugs discovered in animal studies. It was there that I serendipitously or by a stroke of luck discovered the critical importance of the role of carnitine in the human heart. Carnitine is a natural and very safe substance found in most human cells that, by increasing fat metabolism, produces lots of energy. It has a high concentration in the heart and muscles. And, my grandson, please take note that the highest concentration is found in sperm. Also, please take note that I, at age 85, have been taking it daily since 1965! I don't think your father knows about this.

It took me over twenty years with the help of my late friend and partner, Claudio Cavazza, the owner of Sigma tau Pharmaceuticals in Rome, to obtain FDA or government approval of carnitine for the treatment of Primary Carnitine Deficiency, a fatal disease in children. Boy, did we feel more than good about saving the lives of those kids! We also managed to obtain FDA approval for renal dialysis patients most of whom have total body carnitine deficiency.

Now follow me for this is the second lesson I learned, which led me in 1976 to form FIM, the Foundation for Innovation in Medicine, whose mission is to speed up the discovery of innovative medical therapies, mainly by diminishing the very costly barriers to clinically test them in people. More would then be tested and more medical breakthroughs discovered. Do you follow me? If not, join the crowd, for over the decades few have understood, and because of this cultural ignorance millions have needlessly suffered and died before they should have. When I ask men and women and even those at high levels of academic medicine and government, "When was the last cure?" they are clueless but, puzzlingly, don't seem to care. FYI, except for only a couple of cures, there have been a precious few discovered for a long, long, long time!

Before I go on here's an important but little appreciated unfortunate fact of life. There very are few men and women from science to politics who have a broad vision of their subject matter. Just take a look at our ongoing Covid experience. Where is the credible national leader who can explain to the public the total scene from the risk/benefit of opening our society and the importance of pharmaceuticals to treat the virus instead of relying on vaccines alone? I made an attempt to educate the public regarding the big Covid picture including a rationale for treatment of a clinical study in such patients with carnitine to protect the heart. The post can be found on www.fimdefelice.org.

I have no advice on how to handle the lack of leaders with vision except before you buy into something think of the Italian proverb that my mother often offered, "*Chi va piano va sano e lontano*" or "He that goes slowly, goes wisely and a long way." On the other hand, my father countered with, "He who hesitates is lost." Getting too confusing? Let me settle it, both are correct!

Why do these costly barriers exist? It's a complicated story but, in large part, it has to do with the rise of Consumerism, a word that was extremely popular not too long ago but has strangely disappeared in the language of media, although its pan-cultural influence remains almost everywhere. Consumerism deals with our cultural obsession with safety from kids wearing helmets when riding bicycles to safe places for emotionally sensitive students in universities. Regarding clinical studies, our concern with the safety of volunteers was way, way and remains way overblown. Because of the many rules and regulations the costs to conduct them can only be met by those with deep financial pockets.

Let me give you one example of my many personal experiences dealing with clinical research. Prison volunteers were often employed in early clinical research studies. As I said before, if it weren't for such volunteers carnitine would never have been discovered. When I was at WRAIR, I was responsible for designing and supervising early clinical studies of drugs such as anti-malarials and anti-radiation ones for the first time in prison volunteers at the Harry Truman Research Institute in Kansas City, Missouri and the Joliet Prison somewhere in Illinois. In all three situations I got to know the prisoners fairly well and, by the way, learned a lot about their lives just talking with them. It was a rewarding and learning experience for me. Many were real proud to volunteer for research in order to help the sick or prevent illness. I'll never forget how two of those guys approached me with expanded proud chests who had volunteered for a potential anti-malaria drug. Both had brothers in the Vietnam War and were hopeful that their volunteering for the study would come up with a new therapy. This was one of the many times that these male prisoners were proud as hell to volunteer. It was a rewarding, altruistic experience for them to be able to help others. But what happened? The consumerists effectively convinced the FDA to shut down prison studies because the poor guys were bribed or were somehow coerced into volunteering as "guinea pigs" for the very dangerous clinical studies which wasn't at all true. Sure there's risk in everything we do from riding a bike to skiing and the unexpected does occasionally occur. But I know how to design and conduct clinical studies, and these were relatively safe. Nevertheless, the prisoners lost their privilege of performing a noble, courageous and altruistic act for others which tangibly lifted their spirits. Also, to repeat, such studies were relatively inexpensive and conducting them elsewhere was very expensive where only big money could afford them. These high costs eliminate most young creative doctors from testing their ideas. Who pays the price? The actual or future patient!

Here's a carnitine story that has both a serious and humorous side. I couldn't afford to sponsor an intravenous clinical study to evaluate its safety in our country. Fortunately, I had a high level contact in Dr. Stoyan Jeretin, Professor of Anesthesiology at the University of Ljubljana in then communist Yugoslavia, who readily agreed to perform the study. He was also one of the doctors of General Tito, the controversial leader of that country at that time.

So I flew to Yugoslavia with lots of vials of carnitine in my suitcase where he and I designed the clinical study protocol. He was a highly intelligent man and a pleasure to work with. I was surprised and gratified to learn that he, along with his staff, including the nurses, had all volunteered for the study. It really pleased me. They were wonderful altruistic people. Also, they were free to volunteer without government control, unlike in our country.

I returned home before the study started and anxiously awaited the results. About a week later, I got a call from Dr. Jeretin giving me the bad news. All the volunteers, including the good doctor, developed significant phlebitis in their arms which is an inflammation of the veins. Needless to say, that was a big blow for I was counting on the results of this study to move forward in patients with certain medical conditions. I didn't have the patience or money to sponsor another study with a new carnitine intravenous formulation so I took a chance and made a bold decision. I decided to dilute the current formulation in order to reduce its concentration and inject it into myself and volunteers from my staff in my Manhattan office on Madison Avenue.

Boy, was that wishful thinking! I gathered my staff into the large conference room and asked for those who would be volunteers to raise their hands. None did except for my Director of Clinical Studies, Dr. Neil Sanzari. In fact, a few panicked and fled the room which both surprised and amused me. In front of the staff with dropped jaws, he injected me first, and then we waited awhile to see if any immediate toxicity would follow. None happened, so I injected him and both of us experienced no toxic effects. Encouraged by the results in only two volunteers, I launched my first study in Brazil in patients with shock, which is another story written about in Mannion's book.

Now here's the humorous side of the story: on the day following my arrival at Ljubljana, I experienced a little jet lag and told Dr. Jeretin I needed a break and went to an outdoor café not too far from the university to have a cappuccino where I would enjoy one of my favorite pastimes– observing people. After my first few sips I couldn't believe my eyes! Woman after woman strolled by my table, and a significant number of them had bodies that were replicas of Sophia Loren's. You probably don't know who she is but she was a tall, statuesque sensual Italian actress with class, a quality difficult to define. Look her up on your computer. Anyway, the women kept coming and coming even on my walk back to the hotel where I couldn't help observing them. I wondered whether I was suffering from some unusual type of hallucinogenic-induced jet lag.

Later on, Dr. Jeretin called me at my hotel and said, "Steve, let's go to the Alps to have some fresh fish for dinner." And so we did. It was a small restaurant housed in a small mansion at the base of the mountains with a stream nearby. The fish were freshly caught from the stream and deliciously cooked in three different ways.

At dinner, I mentioned my Sophia Loren hallucinogenic experience to him and was awaiting his smile. It never came. He, with a serious look on his face, leaned toward me and said, "What you saw was real. The women here are statuesque, buxom and sensual. Why do you think I was not impressed with American women while I was training in anesthesiology in New York City? There is no comparison!" Then curious as hell, I asked about the genetic origins of these women. He crisply responded, "What genes? It's not a matter of genes; it's the Yugoslavian potatoes!" Initially, I thought he was joking, but he was as serious as can be.

Well, you know that your grandfather couldn't leave Yugoslavia without the potatoes and purchased a small amount of them in order to have them scientifically analyzed in an attempt to discover the nutraceutical "Loren Factor." With Jeretin's connections I had no difficulty getting by Yugoslavian custom inspectors, but it was a different story in the United States. I pleaded with the customs officer about this potentially new scientific discovery, but he insisted that fresh produce was not permitted to enter our country. He, with a funny-looking smile on his face, took the bag from me and said he was sorry but, of course, I didn't believe him.

That night at dinner I told Grandma that I was sure that the wife of the U.S. customs officer would be having those potatoes every night for as long as they lasted! To tell the truth, Grandma was a little skeptical of my story.

She joined me on my next trip to Ljubljana. We were in Austria having lunch in Klagenfurt when I decided we should try to make it through the Alps to Lake Bled in Yugoslavia before sundown. I drove fast like a European, and we arrived at the base of the Alps right about sundown. We came upon the Yugoslavian Communist border patrol, and they asked me to step out of the car. None could speak English that well which created problems. I wrote down the name and phone number of Dr. Jeretin. They made the call, smiled and signaled me to go on.

Now, you're not going to believe what happened. After we descended from the Alps we arrived at the city, Lake Bled. The first sign we saw posted read, *American Gambling Casino*. And what a surprise it was for at that time Yugoslavia was part of the communist Soviet Union behind the impenetrable Iron Curtain where the practice of capitalism was strictly forbidden. But Tito was a rebel, had *cojones* and bent the rules. Grandma and I exchanged mischievous glances and, though we never seriously gambled before, decided to give it a try. We went to the blackjack table where, for some reason, Grandma knew how to play. I then bought some gambling chips, and after Grandma taught me the rules, I grabbed a handful and placed them on the table and asked the *croupier* to deal me a card. I'll never forget the look on his face for he remained motionless and just stared at me. During this weird moment of stillness, the man sitting next to me leaned toward my right ear and whispered, "Sir, you have placed slot machine coins on the table." Grandma and I burst out laughing, but strangely enough the other players remained smile-less. Gambling is a serious game, indeed.

To make a long story short, surprisingly I had a stroke of luck and won a few thousand dollars. When Grandma took my place, she won a few hundred bucks after which she urged that we should quit while we were ahead. But I, excited as hell, decided to bet it all one last time at one shot and lost the gamble. I then had a moment of introspection and concluded that I'd never gamble again. I loved the thrill of it too much and somehow understood the pathology of many high-risk gamblers.

For the record, it took a gourmet dinner with fine wine, and violins playing in the background before Grandma forgave me for losing the money.

At Ljubljana we visited the same café for cappuccino and did our people watching. After about five minutes observing the many Loren women, Grandma looked at me and burst out into laughter and said, "Steve, I must admit you're right!" Sophia after Sophia passed by our sidewalk table for as long as we were there. The smile on Grandma's face suddenly disappeared, and she commanded, "Steve, you are never going to come to Ljubljana again." And I never did!

Here's an interesting historical point. The statuesque and beautiful wife of former President Trump, Melania, was from Yugoslavia and attended the University of Ljubljana. Though it's highly improbable, if we ever should meet, I'd like to learn more about these potatoes!

Let me tell you another story about a doctor with balls or *cojones* at the University of Pennsylvania. I've met a few in my career, and we need more of them these days where everyone now is looking over your shoulders. Whistle blowers are now everywhere! My father had a life-threatening block in his carotid artery which is the major artery that supplies blood and oxygen to the brain. He also had a very weak heart and the doctor, who was a surgeon along with the anesthesiologist, were justifiably concerned that he might not survive the operation. But there was no choice but to go forward with it for, if not, he would suffer a crippling or fatal stroke. I decided that if he did run into cardiac problems due to a lack of oxygen, the administration of high dose intravenous carnitine might pull him through.

I met with the surgeon before the operation and reviewed the previous carnitine studies with him. He was a distinguished looking man with steely, confident eyes. He listened attentively and asked me to leave the studies with him to further digest. He called me a few days later and agreed that I could come to the operating room with my vials of intravenous carnitine along with a syringe, and if my father ran into serious trouble I would be the one to administer it to him. Needless to say, I appreciated his courageous act. I did check it out with my father. He smiled broadly, held my hand and said, "Go ahead, son." Somehow the touch of his hands was more reassuring than the sound of his words. Though I'm not sure of this, I think the surgeon didn't tell the operating team who I was and why I was there holding a syringe and vials standing by the operating table. I remembered the looks of the team members which came back to me years later after Robert Redford asked Paul Newman, "Who are those guys?" when they were being tracked down by a posse in the movie, Butch Cassidy and the Sundance Kid.

Anyway, my father pulled though without the need of carnitine. Now, balls or no balls, medical situations such as this could not be done today because of our over concern with safety. The doctor would be mercilessly exposed by informers and barred from medical practice. Today, I would have to spend a small fortune in order to satisfy the onerous rules and regulations before I, as a physician, could administer a single, extremely safe natural substance to my own father in order to try to save his life.

Let me wrap it up regarding three complicated attempts to encourage more clinical research mainly because of the lessons learned by my carnitine experience. It's complicated, so take a break, take a walk and clear your head.

The first is the Orphan Drug Act. A patent grants you an exclusive right to own an invention or discovery. If, for example, you own an idea or invention and have a patent, you would spend money to develop it because you have no competition and can hopefully make a profit. Remember, money is a big understandable motivator to take risks. Natural substances like carnitine are, however, difficult to patent but I did manage to obtain a few. The Orphan Drug Act also grants some type of ownership to a natural substance. Because of my patents and the Act, Dr. Claudio Cavazza helped finance carnitine studies to obtain FDA approval for children and dialysis patients.

The second is my Nutraceutical Research and Education Act or NREA which deals mainly with dietary supplements that are available at the drug and health food stores without a prescription. (FYI, for reasons too complicated to explain here, carnitine is both a pharmaceutical and dietary supplement.) And, they are generally not patented because they are natural substances and, for that reason, few costly clinical studies are done to show whether they are safe and effective. They were sold, and still are, mainly by clever marketing techniques as is done with soaps and perfumes.

Now back then before you were born, I based the NREA on the same principles of the Orphan Drug Act. Congressman Frank Pallone, a Democrat and now Chairman of the House Energy and Commerce Committee, attended one of my FIM's Nutraceutical conferences at the internationally famous Waldorf Astoria hotel in Manhattan where our presidents used to stay before the Chinese bought it. I once spent a night in the presidential suite where, if my aging brain serves me right, there were seven bedrooms. What happened there is a secret that I'll take to the grave next to beautiful Grandma DeFelice and won't dare to tell her even after I leave Purgatory a couple of thousand years from now and meet her in Heaven!

Well, I and Congressman Pallone, a very bright and good man, got together to discuss the pros and cons of the NREA. He was convinced of its importance because it would encourage clinical research on dietary supplements to evaluate their effectiveness and safety, and he boldly introduced the NREA in Congress. For certain reasons, there was not a single group to support it, and the effort rapidly died for reasons I've written about in the past on my website. FYI, bottom line, it's all about money, power, self-interest and self-deception.

But surprisingly, FIM's efforts did persuade certain companies and even the government to sponsor clinical studies on a number of them. Unfortunately, most studies had negative results. The reason? I believe that the body doesn't use them if they are not needed or it may be due to the faulty design of the studies lacking creativity—which I've also written about. Clinical studies or not, the public continues to consume them more than ever. Why do you think this is so? Remember ersatz gods?

Before going on, I forgot to mention that I coined the term 'nutraceuticals' and have been acknowledged of having done so in multiple media outlets such as the New York Times, who called me the *Don Quixote of Nutraceuticals,* and in William Safire's On Language Column in the Times Magazine section. FYI, I've been on a number of television shows such as Good Morning America and The Today Show speaking about the importance of clinical research.

Now here's a fact that would make you proud of your grandfather. I'm probably the only person you know or whomever you will know who has added a new word to the English dictionary. I coined the term nutraceutical while walking on the famous public square, Piazza Navona, in Rome not far from the Trevi Fountain, after a wonderful dinner coupled with, may I say, lots of wonderful wine at one of my favorite Italian restaurants whose name, as of now, disturbingly eludes my aging brain. The word is now in the Oxford English Dictionary where I am personally credited for coining the term as well as in other dictionaries and mentioned on many websites.

And now to the Big Kahuna—Doctornauts! Way back in 1972, my first book, *Drug Discovery: The Pending Crisis* was published. In it I proposed that, in order to avoid our irrational concern with safety, physicians should be able to take more risks in volunteering for clinical studies than anybody else so more potential therapies could be tested. After all, they know more about the promise and side effects of the drugs being tested than others and, in addition, it would be an altruistic, noble act of courage which I believe should be the right of doctors to help their patients.

Well, you wouldn't believe it! On the book media tour I was accused of being like the cruel, sadistic doctors in concentration camps during World War II who, as I mentioned before, mercilessly killed and also experimented on men, women and children as guinea pigs. They often ripped the fetuses from the wombs of their mothers and then, to complete the act, stabbed the helpless creatures with their bayonets. Let me tell you that it wasn't a very pleasant experience–not at all! But, like Frankenstein and lightning, this experience once more strengthened my resolve to move forward on a long and costly, and it was very costly, journey to persuade Congress to enact the Doctornaut Act. I coined the word 'doctornaut' in order to give the mission an identifiable and specific identity which hopefully would more easily attract public attention. I decided to start out with a costly physician survey asking them whether they would agree to be doctornauts on natural substances. Over 50 percent of male and female doctors responded in the affirmative, a highly positive result. Armed with this result, I decided to first enlist the support of the 50 highly respected U.S. and international physicians on my Advisory Board with high level contacts whom I knew personally to support the Doctornaut Act. Included on my Board were Louis Lasagna, the world's leading spokesman on the importance of clinical research and Michael DeBakey, the world's most famous heart surgeon.

What followed was one of the most disappointing and puzzling reactions by my prestigious colleagues. There was not only a general lack of enthusiasm and support, but the few that did so were lukewarm in their support. There, however, was one outstanding exception. William Thornton at the University of Texas, who was a doctor-astronaut who experimented on himself while in outer space, enthusiastically supported the Doctornaut Act.

I would have surrendered the ship if it wasn't for Grandma DeFelice, who gave me hell and pushed me to continue my journey. And so I did for a couple of more decades hiring a couple public relations firms, another personal costly endeavor, without success. By the way, over the years FIM never received a penny of support from anyone or anywhere and all expenses came out of my pocket. I never told your father about it, for when I go to Purgatory there will be less money in his inheritance.

To repeat, we have an unbudgeable cultural blind spot to the critical importance of clinical research and things weren't encouraging. And then some real good news surprisingly came my way. Through my political contacts I managed to get an appointment with both physician and then Senate Majority Leader, Bill Frist. Boy, was I excited for I was convinced that my long journey might finally be coming to the end and new medical discoveries and cures might soon be coming our way. For your information, the Senate Majority Leader has a very powerful position regarding passing new legislation. But before the meeting I had an idea. On my FIM Board was physician, Ted Lewers, the Chairman of the powerful American Medical Association or AMA, who was supportive of the Doctornaut Act. If I could get the support of the AMA, this would really impress and encourage Senator Frist. I emphasized to Dr. Lewers that medicine was becoming too much of a business and wouldn't it be wonderful if doctors would courageously step to the plate and take risks in order to accelerate the discovery of cures for their patients.

The result? Zero interest which really bothered me for I still naively believe it's the responsibility of physicians, not scientists or political figures, to lead in the medical arena.

Well, my meetings with Senator Frist went better than I had hoped because he needed no convincing regarding the critical importance of clinical research to make medical discoveries, and he readily agreed to pursue the Doctornaut Act. He, as a first step to evaluate the receptivity of the Act by his Senate colleagues and major health institutions, circulated a draft of the Act. The result? Zero support–and I mean zero!

Well, my grandchildren, instead of strengthening Frankenstein, this electric lightning bolt killed him. I gave up the ship except for a few minor attempts. I decided to submit an op-ed piece to one of the most prestigious newspapers in the world. And it was accepted which letter of acceptance I have somewhere in my vast files. Wow, I felt reborn. Silence then ensued, and then I discovered the paper would not publish it. Why? I don't know but probably the editor spoke to his medical consultants who nixed the idea. It's that damn cultural blind spot again.

Before going on, I'd like to point out that Senator Frist is an ignored medical visionary. When I began my crusade to warn against the oncoming of biological warfare, I wasn't aware that he, with much more clout, also warned against this threat when he was in the Senate and also more recently as a private citizen. President George W. Bush recognized this threat and lent some support to prepare for it. But the general interest was minimal and the effort to do something about it was therefore, also minimal.

And now, Olivia and Stephen Carlos, I'll try to offer you some advice regarding ways to adapt to the new controlling technological world. I know you don't drink, but I would suggest that you gulp down a glass of wine before you read what I have to say.

Chapter 11

GRANDPA'S WORDS OF WISDOM

Your Grandfather has reluctantly concluded that the Technological Revolution, fueled by the Internet Democracy permitting the free expression of the Six Human Characteristics will, in one way or another, lead to the loss of your freedom by the domination of cultural evil beings brought about by almost total government control over your lives. As we have seen, it's already happening, and you're at the crossroads of the disappearance of the traditional world and entering into the technological one. Our culture and public mind are now largely engulfed and controlled by national hysteria, an extremely emotional, self-sustaining and invasive power where attempts at reasoning are taking a back seat. But we can't even depend on reason. Cervantes wrote that, "Reason is the greatest madness." It can be used to justify all kinds of behavior. As I mentioned before, because of the human capacity to abusively employ both emotion and reason, our Founding Fathers established the three parts of government in our Constitution as a balancing act against having too much power in a single person or institution. Despite the current attack on our country, we are trying to stem the tide of people wanting to come here whereas Russia is trying to keep people from leaving. Why do you think this is so? Turn to your Emoji brain for the answer.

(Speaking of Cervantes, he died on the same day as Shakespeare. Thomas Jefferson and John Adams, both signers of the Constitution, died on the same day, July 4th, Aldous Huxley and C.S. Lewis, two of our most influential modern thinkers, also died on the same day, but unfortunately their departure went virtually unnoticed because it was right about the time of President Kennedy's assassination.)

Religion, family and patriotism are fast fading being inexorably replaced by the interplay of self-deception or rationalization, power-money, recognition, self-interest, competition and the persistent yet big loser, altruism. They are operational everywhere as never before!

The good news is that the future is not, as in mathematics, predictable and perhaps things will turn out well. Maybe there's a Plato's philosopher king or even a philosopher queen somewhere on the horizon. Maybe some charismatic leader will emerge from the religious world. There's also a possibility that a catastrophic event will bring our divided country together again. These are real possibilities. But, unfortunately, you can't count on them, so it's critical to find ways to adapt to your loss of freedom. Or should you? There is the serious option for both of you to go with the flow and just let things happen. For example, would you be willing to take the daily *soma* happy morning pill or have a brain computer chip inserted which, by using neurotechnology, can find out what you're thinking and straighten things out provided by the government? Tempting, isn't it? Grandpa DeFelice ain't built that way and, smart or futilely dumb, would mightily try to maintain his independence. And the way to do this would be to take Yogi Berra's fork in the road advice by taking it–taking the good with you from the traditional world and bringing it into the technological one. Remember how the great Dostoevsky defined a human being. "Man is a creature who can adapt to any situation."

But before offering advice on how to adapt and blend both worlds, I think it's important for you to have a belief on what is the meaning of life.

One of the most mysterious answers to this question was proposed by Professor Ali Shakrani, our friend and close relative of then King Hussein of Jordan. Patricia Park and I were having lunch with him at Trump Towers when the subject came up. He paused in deep thought and then launched into what seemed like an endless story. It was about a man who was searching for the meaning of life by visiting place after place, asking many supposedly wise men what was the answer to the riddle. Finally, with sudden revelatory eyes and the broadest of smiles, the man finally found the answer to the riddle. It was, "Life is a fountain." We also smiled, but not as broadly, nodded our heads in appreciation, while not having the slightest idea regarding the answer. So we decided to conduct some research and here's the story: *A man sold all his possessions and left his family to travel the world, because he wanted to know the meaning of life. After many years of seeking, and near despair, his last hope was a guru who lived high up on a very dangerous mountain. Up the mountain our seeker went, through a thunderstorm, tired and desperate and hungry—his food was all gone, he injured one foot but struggled on with a cane out of a tree branch. Finally, on top of the mountain, there sat the guru, surrounded by tame animals, with bright sunlight breaking through a hole in the clouds to shine all around him.*

The seeker staggered forward. "O holy guru, I have given up everything to seek the truth, but it will all be worthwhile if you can answer my question: What is the meaning of life?"

The guru smiled and said, "My son, here is the answer you seek: Life is a fountain." After a long pause, the seeker shook his head. "A fountain? I have come thousands of miles to hear your words—my possessions are all gone, I'm starving, I'll probably die on this mountain—and all you have to say is, life is a fountain?" The guru trembled. "You mean…it's not a fountain?"

Can you figure it out? If so, let us know!

Answers to the meaning of life are many varying from culture-to-culture and even town-to-town. In Ecclesiastes it is written that, "Life is meaningless." In many Christian religions the critical importance of faith, good works and charity give life meaning as a path to Heaven.

During the famous period of Enlightenment where many great philosophers and scientists were born, and though they proposed a wide variety of significantly different views of life such as Isaac Newton, an interesting religious man, and Voltaire, an atheist, most, however, agreed that the fundamental goal or meaning of life is to find happiness.

Do you remember when I asked you, *Uhai ni nini* in Swahili, an African language, regarding what's the meaning of life? Though inadequate, we came up with, "To wake up in the morning and look forward to the day" which implied being happy. Surprisingly, practically all to whom I spoke to were impressed by the definition. But caveat emptor! Don't forget that the sociopathic, monster killer, Stalin, woke up in the morning and looked forward to his happy days. Or maybe not.

This was one of my favorite answers. At the grocery store when I was checking out I asked the clerk what was the meaning of life. She paused and then answered, "How the hell do I know? Why don't you Google it!"

Now let's take a look at your Grandfather's suggestions, if, to repeat you want to maintain some semblance of who you are.

The first is to know who you are, who the other folks are and where you are. Even in the traditional world only a small parentage of men and women are capable of managing these disciplines which are core in maintaining one's individual freedom. That's why there are leaders from the family to the government to help guide human behavior be they good or bad ones. So how do you acquire these three disciplines and stick to them? It's by developing the habit of being totally alone with yourself which is increasingly difficult to do because of our increasingly thrombosed calendars. I would suggest taking a weekly walk alone without any way to contact the outer world and just let your mind flow even if there's something on your mind that needs clearing up. I naturally had this habit before my teens, so it was easy for me, but with your cell phones you have to work at it and discipline yourselves.

As you know, I've travelled much of the world and really looked forward to walking the cities alone. I would try to handle my meetings during the day and only had business dinners when necessary. My favorite walking cities were New York, Paris and Rome where, when walking, I just thought, observed and had a sense of humanity. London was too spread-out to get in sync. Do you remember the little cabin that I bought on top of a mountain in the heavy forest? It was my place to experience pure solitude where I sensed something beyond humanity. Somehow, a writer from the New York Times got wind of me and the cabin and wrote an article that was published in that newspaper. In it I observed that silence or solitude in the forest differs from silence in a home. Though not necessary, part of that message is to get out of the house where your mind can flow more freely.

Here are two thoughts that might encourage you to discipline yourselves to take the walk. The first is that when in contemplative solitude, there understandably arise many painful thoughts and problems to confront which have, according to Confucius, a highly positive side to it. He said, "Pain makes man think; thought makes man wise and wisdom makes man

111

happy." The second is, when fully developed, being in thoughtful solitude is extremely pleasurable.

The following are some quotes on solitude or being alone that I found in my notes that support my thoughts:

Solitude has its own strange beauty to it.

Solitude is independence.

It is only in solitude that I find my inner core.

Developing the habit of being alone is the essential foundation to build upon if you want to maintain enough independence to be yourselves. If you are not willing or too weak, then you'll have no choice but to go with the flow and become a voluntary slave.

There are other schools of thought regarding the importance of solitude and meditation. The most famous one was *premeditatio malorum* or premeditation of the worse happenings in one's life proposed by the Stoic Roman, Seneca such as disease, torture, betrayal and war. He claims that it will make you stronger to confront life's travails. Now I hope he practiced what he preached. Roman Emperor Nero, for some reason, ordered Seneca to commit suicide by cutting his arm artery and slowly bleeding to death, a not uncommon custom in those days. His loving wife decided to join him and also cut her artery. Nero got wind of the latter and sent his troops to stop his wife from her suicidal attempt. But Seneca couldn't bleed enough to die so he asked for a poison, which I think was the hemlock that Socrates drank. But, poor guy, that didn't work either! Nero lost his patience and sent his troops where they placed him in a hot water bath where he somehow suffocated.

Speaking of Nero, he was one of the most cruel and evil of the Roman emperors, and ordered the death of St. Paul, the famous missionary of the New Testament. Now St. Paul was a Roman citizen, and Roman law prohibited him from being crucified so Nero had him beheaded.

Grandchildren, I would not recommend *premeditatio malorum*.

But I'll somewhat take back this recommendation. Aquinas and others believed that meditation on one's death will make you appreciate the good things in life and, by doing so, become stronger. I developed this habit as a teenager up to today. Have you ever done it? If not, I would strongly recommend it.

Now let's turn to the eroding Judeo-Christian based religions such as Catholicism and the many Protestant ones. Except for highly focused religious media outlets, little, and I mean little, is mentioned of God, Christ and the path to eternal life. Your mother is a very religious Catholic and made sure you attended religious instruction classes when you were very young where you were supposed to learn about the rituals of Baptism, Communion and Confirmation. A couple of years ago when I asked you what were the messages behind each sacred ritual your responses were blank faces and silence.

Now I understand this, for nowhere in your and others total culture can you readily find mentions of God and Christianity, let alone the existence of sin and eternal life. There is little reinforcement of such beliefs to be found. So what are you supposed to do? Forget about it, or give it some deep serious thought?

It's up to you to make the choice, but I would urge you to learn more about it and keep it seriously in mind because it has a value in at least handling the trials and tribulations of life. I can vouch for that based on my intense religious searchings and beliefs when I was a young man.

As a start, as I describe in the God chapter, there is far, far more persuasive intellectual evidence based on the arguments presented for the existence of a personal God than against his existence. Unfortunately, you will find them difficult to find elsewhere, but the intellectual attraction is only the first step in your quest. For the thing called faith is what will bring you there, and the only way to obtain it is by developing the habit of prayer. And you must "will" it to get there. The advice of the old Catholic theologians sums it up. *Intelligo ut credam* or *I understand in order to believe*, and *Credo ut Intelligam*, or *I believe in order to understand*.

What's interesting to note, and, in a sense prophetic, is that many Christian sects are predicting that all the warning signs of today point to Armageddon in Israel, the final battle between the Devil and God found in Revelations in the New Testament which will end the world. Though the good news is that God will win, the bad news is that lots of people will be destined for Hell.

Practically all Christianity since the time of Jesus Christ believes that faith in him and his teachings are necessary to enter the kingdom of God. My grandson and your cousin, Maximilian, is nearing the age of 30, and went through both a traumatic childhood and early adult phase of his life. Not too long ago, he found Jesus as well as his wife, Tara, whom he loves. He now has three young daughters, Brielle, Kinsley and Harlow who are, for your information, my great grandchildren. He told me to urge both of you to seek and love Jesus and, by the way, he believes along with the multimillions of others that Armageddon is very near.

Just a note about Jesus before I go on: a number of talented modern scholars are increasingly looking into the life of Jesus and whether the Bible fits the requirements of a truly historic document. For example, was Jesus married or did he die on the cross, let alone return to life three days later? But it's very important to note that none questions his existence as well as many of his teaching parables including his claim that he was divine. The great Christian intellect, C.S. Lewis, claimed that he was either the Son of God or a madman. My Emoji brain tells me that the fact that billions of Christians believe in the former is something to be intellectually highly respected and considered.

The great Christian and mathematical intellect and one of my favorite minds, Pascal, proposed the famous Pascal's Wager of probability which states that you have nothing to lose by believing in the Christian God, even if he doesn't exist, because if he does and you are a sinner, you know where you are heading after death, and you don't want to go there. But, if he does exist, then you hit the jackpot!

Bottom line, it's your call, but there's no doubt that such faith is a shield against the tyranny of the technological revolution. Think about religion while you're taking your walks in your solitude. And, don't forget, you can also pray while walking as well as on your knees!

You may be wondering why I've not addressed the beautiful thing called love. There are many uses and definitions of this word, but I wanted to save it specifically for the love experienced and shared in families, which defies verbal definition, but which your Emoji brains readily perceive. I can't conceive how it would be to grow up in a family without love which is almost becoming commonplace today due, in large part, to the forces of technology. To repeat, I cannot conceive of it! Pope Benedict said that every child needs a father and mother which imply the power of the beauty of love which is essential to confront the disquieting storms of life. But his words were totally ignored by the media.

Why do you think this is so?

Regarding the family, the fading of the traditional family is what bothers me the most for that's where you really learn about what life's all about, including love. All six human characteristics daily come into play from awakening to bedtime where, by experiencing them, you learn to adapt to life by being accommodating to others, particularly when relatives are close by. Thus, if someone has a financial problem, the family chips in. If one of the daughters behaves like a horse's ass, she is reprimanded and set straight. G.K. Chesterton, an ardent champion of the traditional family, described it as everyone being together interacting with each other with no or little government interference. Of course, this is no longer so due to technology. I just learned that a close, divorced female relative of your father who worked at many jobs to support her kids and send them to college has been deserted by her children. One son lives in Asia, one daughter in the Middle East and the other daughter keeps changing places somewhere far away. She's, compounded by Covid, now an isolated and lonely woman. Yes, her kids communicate by Zoom which is a wonderful way of getting rid of their guilt and responsibility to be close to their mother in order to care for her both emotionally and when the diseases of the aging hit her. She has no other relatives close by. Do you remember Uncle Jimmy and Uncle Benny?

Remember, actions speak louder than words!

Now, you may incorrectly believe you still live in a traditional family. Not true. Your father has no close relatives and your mother's are all spread out in our country and Mexico. And, both of you will soon be geographically separated from your parents and yourselves. Technology, in one way or another, is increasingly separating the family. Will you be close by when the inevitable maladies of aging hit your mother and father? And, are you aware that when you're in trouble anywhere in the world it will be your parents, and no one else, including your friends, who will be somehow, someway by your side? Think about it.

Olivia, have you ever thought about being a married mother and having babies the biologically natural way and rearing children while having a career? Or is having a career what's on your mind and the others can wait for another time, or if not at all? And what about your husband, or can that wait for another time, or maybe not at all? If you intend to

115

marry here are two qualities that you should look for as proposed by the comedian Groucho Marx: "The husband who wants a happy marriage should learn to keep his mouth shut and his checkbook open!" There's more than a kernel of truth in those words, and don't forget, it's nice to be economically comfortable.

Apart from the love showered upon you by your giving mother, it's difficult to find any general celebrations of the beauty of motherhood. Remember that wounded and dying soldiers on the battlefield cry out to be with their mothers. I just read where everyone in a group of Catholic seminarians was highly influenced by their love of the Virgin Mary, the mother of Jesus, to enter the priesthood. And let's not forget that you, your brother, your father, your mother and grandfather were all blessed by loving, giving and sacrificing motherly love. Can you conceive of not having experienced it? I can't.

But it really bothers me to say that disrupting technology is changing the nature of the role of the daughter. In the traditional world a commonly used saying was, "A son is a son until he finds a wife, and a daughter is a daughter for the rest of her life." Olivia, what do you think?

Stephen Carlos, I'm afraid that by expressing my admiration for the beauty of giving mothers, you might have the impression that such admiration applies to women in general. Not so, my grandson. There's a saying regarding women that reads, "You can't live with them, and you can't live without them" which sums it up! They are supreme manipulators and have superior power over men when it comes to getting what they want. Your mother is a classic example. (Don't tell your father!) And today they have taken center stage in practically many sectors. Thus there are Women's Rights, Women's Liberation, Women's Careers, Women's Health and Women in Politics. They are increasingly gaining power, and you must remember wise old Samuel Johnson, who warned, "Nature has given woman so much power that the law cannot afford to give her more" which is happening today. And, may I add, they love to spend money and talk a lot! It's not an accident that the word *tongue* is feminine in Greek, Latin, Spanish, French, Italian and German and other languages. Now don't get me wrong, as I said before, I'm not at all a misogynist. During my broad life's experience I've met all types in many different cultural settings, and I can unequivocally state that I love women.

If you ever get married, I'd like you to know something about your Grandma DeFelice, a wife who was made for me. Despite arguments regarding our children–that's your father and your late Aunt Julia–we experienced a wonderful half-century together. Like your mother, she was a chemistry major. She was president of her class at Chestnut Hill College, and I was president of my Jefferson Medical School fraternity when we met while I was on a ladder decorating my fraternity Christmas tree. She had a blind date with one of my classmates but, after observing her, I quickly eliminated the competition. After graduation and our marriage, she was offered a number of jobs but we decided that it was best for her to stay home, manage the family and develop her talents. She became a superb chef. Just ask your father! After I came home at night from an arduous commute driving from Manhattan, we sat down and had our old-fashioned cocktail together discussing things related to our home life. I never discussed my business. Boy did I enjoy beholding her physical and spiritual beauty and just feeling the calming comfort of being in her presence. After our glasses were empty and with anticipation, a delightful dinner invariably followed. She also became a professional photographer before the digital age and developed her films in the dark room that we built in the basement.

She became a hole-in-one golfer and found select friends on the golf links who were strong, wise, traditional women particularly, though opposite personalities, Mrs. Esther Daniels and Mrs. Louise Ventrella. She was the leader of a group of such delightful women who all had positive outlooks on life arranging for trips to the Manhattan museums, Broadway shows, Lincoln Center ballet, and even to our cabin in the mountains. The ladies didn't appreciate opera, my favorite art form.

My grandson, here is a point to put in your memory bank. You know that I'm not a patient man and sometimes get a wee bit out of control. But Grandma DeFelice was a master manipulator who knew how to calm my agitated waters. If you ever do marry, make sure she's a wise manipulator!

I'm not sure whether both of you know how grandma passed away. There are those who pass suddenly and others who suffer for a longer time. It was the former that happened to my wife. I haven't read the differences on the nature of suffering between the two types and, for some puzzling reason, am not interested.

We were eating at Ferraro's, a local Westfield Italian restaurant, enjoying a hot plate of pasta puttanesca talking about you and where you might be heading in the future. She had recently treated you both to the Christmas Show with the Rockettes at Radio City Music Hall in New York, and you all shared a wonderful experience.

The next night while lying in bed she had a heart attack in the middle of the night. I called 911, and we made it to the hospital after which all thought she had passed the danger zone. Two days later she was gone. Her last words to me were, "Steve, I can't breathe." Below is the obituary that I wrote in the Westfield Leader.

A Remembrance of the Death of Marianne Patrice DeFelice
Stephen L. DeFelice, M.D.

It was on November 22, 2009, about 3 a.m., when I was awakened by a nudge from my wife, Pat. I turned to her, but before I could speak she said, "Steve, I don't feel well." I immediately turned on the light, and she was pale as pale can be. Her body was ice cold and her skin clammy. She said she was nauseated and had diarrhea. I took her blood pressure and it was in the normal range. I then made a preliminary diagnosis of some type of food poisoning or flu. She then vomited and her appearance worsened, bringing back images of two patients I treated in the past who had the same look before a soon-to-come heart attack. I asked her if she had chest pain. She put her hand to her chest and described it to me. Though it wasn't the classic heart attack type, it was enough for me to call 911. The police arrived within a few minutes and the ambulance with the paramedics shortly thereafter. She was now short of breath and very frightened. An electrocardiogram was taken and showed that she was having an early heart attack.

They rushed her to Overlook Hospital and she was immediately taken to the cardiac unit, where a catheter was inserted into the chambers of her heart. Two of her arteries had partial blockages, but one was completely occluded. The latter was removed and her heart showed improvement. That was more than a happy moment. The next day her condition rapidly improved but she still complained of mild chest pain, which disappeared after repeated doses of nitroglycerin. On November 24, 2009, I was by her bedside during the late afternoon. She looked beautiful. Her hair was combed in my favorite way and she turned to makeup to add to her beauty. We schemed to convince the doctor to release her before Thanksgiving. I held her hand and kissed her goodbye. We were happy now, realizing that this was not the end, and we would be together as long as God willed it.

That same evening while I was writing in my study, I received a phone call from the hospital that Pat was having a second heart attack. I sped to the hospital and arrived at the cardiac unit just as she was about to enter. There was an impressive catheter crew of about ten technicians. We all thought that the same or another artery was occluded. Just before the procedure began, I was by her side. She then spoke her last words to me, which will remain in my memory bank until my final moment. "I can't breathe, Steve, I can't breathe." Then I, in return, spoke my last words to my wife. "Don't worry, Pat, when this is over, you'll be okay." But I must confess my intuition had unwelcome doubts.

The anesthesiologist asked me to administer the oxygen while he was setting up his equipment. He told me that she was in congestive heart failure, which further increased my doubts. I placed the oxygen mask over her nose and mouth. She then placed her hand upon my hand that was holding the mask. I sensed by our touching of hands she was happy that I was there by her side. The anesthesiologist then took over. He intubated her trachea in order to ensure a sufficient oxygen supply.

The cardiologist then asked me to step behind a wall with a window, which made it possible to view the entire procedure as well as hear what was said. The catheter was inserted, and I prayed that it would reach the heart chamber in time to remove the clot, saving my wife from death's grasp. Then she underwent cardiac arrest. Three members of the team attempted cardiovascular resuscitation with rapid rhythm pumping down on her chest. They were successful, and I again prayed that she would make it through. Then I heard the cardiologist say, "She has

no anterior chamber," which meant the vital part of her heart that pumps the blood throughout the body was not functioning.

Pat once more went into cardiac arrest and the team once more tried to resuscitate her. There was little success, so a heart stimulant was then injected into her heart muscle. That failed. The pumping on the chest vigorously resumed, and I was sure that a number of her ribs were now fractured. I entered the room and both the cardiologist and I concluded that there was no hope. He ordered the team to stop.

My wife of 48 years was now dead. The entire cardiac team left the room, and I was now alone with Pat. You may find this tough to believe, but for the first couple of minutes I don't remember what I thought and felt. Perhaps that was due to the fact I did not think or feel. Then it struck me. The immensity and unbelievability of it all. And then the mystery of it all. Pat was alive one moment and gone the next. I walked to her body, lifted her upper torso, hugged her and wept mightily. Her body, covered with large discolored areas caused by bleeding in the skin, was still warm.

I cast aside my scientific knowledge and hoped there still was a chance that she could hear. I told her how much I love her and how my life will not be the same without her. Shortly after, my son, Stephen, and my grandson, Maximilian, who both loved her as I did, with a love that cannot be surpassed, arrived. We all gazed upon our beautiful Pat, refusing to accept the reality of her death. We took turns kissing her, holding her hand, speaking words of love and sad farewell. There were no dry eyes in that room.

I made a decision to make a one-on-one final goodbye. I gently lifted her closed eyelids – one at a time – and placed my eyes close to hers. They were still moist and still radiating beauty as they did before her death. I gently lowered the eyelids back in place, realizing that I had just seen my wife's eyes for the last time.

I then whispered in her ears and once more spoke of our love and how magnificent a wife she was. Though the intubation tube was still in place, I managed to push it aside and successfully had our farewell kiss. It was a long and passionate one. Her lips were still warm. My imagination convinced me that she actually returned my kiss. Or maybe it wasn't just my imagination! Stephen, Max and I together bid her farewell. As we were walking down the corridors of the hospital, we all were asking ourselves, "Why? It just doesn't make sense."

At home we sat around, sometimes in silence and sometimes in tears. I drank cognac until I could drink no more. Others, besides family members, will sorely miss the presence of Pat. Over the years, she has touched many lives in many different positive ways. "Warm, caring, giving, generous, always helping others, wonderful to be with, an angel, selfless," among others, have been expressed to me since her death a few days ago. She was indeed an extraordinary woman. Fate smiled upon me when I met her for the first time trimming a Christmas tree at a party at my medical fraternity. My friend and

I both had blind dates. Pat was his date and her friend was mine. Needless to say, this arrangement was quickly reversed that night, and that's when our romance began.

...

As you know, I live in a large home with many rooms containing poignant memories of her existence, and I visited them all. Strangely enough, I initially didn't feel that sorry for myself, but what saturated my mind and even angered me was the existential mystery of how such a beautiful creature comes into being and how she's with you one day and gone the next, which took me once more to thinking about God and the possible afterlife. And, by the way, I remember thinking about how you two missed out on having a beautiful and exceptionally wise grandmother.

Instead of seeking solace from others, including family, I became a total recluse with no desire, in fact, an aversion, to speak or see anyone. I, instead, read a lot, drank a lot—and I'm not talking about soda water—and concentrated on my writings. I lost contact with many of them. It's interesting to note that, generally speaking, women have a greater capacity to love then men, but it's also interesting to note that women accommodate much better to the deaths of their husbands then the other way around.

Then enters Patricia Park, or better known to you as Miss Pat. Pat was, and remains, a beautiful, highly intelligent, kind and patient woman with an exceptional gift to read people and situations. In her youth she was a member of the National Honor Society and also Phi Beta Kappa at Skidmore College, during which time, as a romance language major, she lived awhile in Paris. She's a member of The Daughters of the American Revolution because her ancestor, John McKitrick, fought in the army under George Washington during the Revolution. She joined my company at age twenty-two in 1974 and learned Italian. She became a supreme diplomat dealing with many national and international leaders related to my company including hosting the chief general of a large Middle East air force along with his family. They never forgot it. Though she won't admit it, I'm pretty sure that the great tenor, Luciano Pavarotti, was after her. One main problem was that many of our male relationships of various types were chasing her, but she somehow diplomatically managed to fend them off.

In a real sense she became my "right-hand man," helping me achieve my career objectives. She's a natural leader, as exemplified when a dozen of her Skidmore classmates showed up in Manhattan to celebrate her 60th birthday, during which she was interviewed on the national Good Morning America television show. She reared a good and successful son, James, a Villanova graduate, who specializes in global advanced corporate financial technology and is studying for his MBA at NYU. He, because of Covid, has been working remotely for a large international firm, and living in the family's New Hampshire home for the last year with his attractive honeybun, Jennifer, along with Sadie, an odd-looking dog.

Speaking of her family, tragedy seems to be forever present. She, constantly by his side, personally took care of her father, Jack Park, a good man, who slowly suffered and passed away because of lung disease. She took on the same missions with her mother, Ellie, and her younger sister Nancy who both, after prolonged battles with cancer, joined her father. Her sister lived in California, and Pat flew to her side to be with her for a month and help her, particularly in her agonizing final days. During Nancy's last struggling night Pat, while holding her hand, read from the Book of Psalms in the Old Testament beginning with the 23rd. She's now managing her 98 year-old aunt with dementia, no easy task. Now think of this. If Pat weren't around, who would have taken care of them?–for there were no other family members up to the job. And what about the future when the technological family becomes permanent?

After grandma's death, Pat still helped me with my foundation, consulting jobs and, thank God, helped manage my home obligations and functions which I despise. We became very close, and I asked her, and she accepted, to be my girlfriend–not companion! I'm a lucky guy, for I know a number of widowers who live alone, and they are not to be envied.

Before I go on, here's an interesting story about technology that, though humorous, says a lot more. Medical doctor Aram Chobanian, who was President of Boston University and a good man, my friend and member of my Advisory Committee, told me a story about a talk given by Isaac Asimov, an accomplished distinguished science fiction author. Mr. Asimov speculated that future technology would permit humans to live forever. He paused, gazed intently at the audience and asked, "Those of you who are married, could you live with your spouse for 1,000 years?" The initial audience response was hearty laughter, but Dr. Chobanian sensed there was a second, subtle muted reaction when the men and women began to give it some serious thought. What do you think they were thinking?

FYI, the jellyfish, *Turritopsis dohrnii,* is apparently immortal.

And now to my final point that I want you to take very seriously for you'll need it more than ever: it's networking. Networking means making connections to others to mutually benefit yourself and the others. In other words, you scratch my back, and I'll scratch yours. You're probably wondering why this is so important. It's simple. As I said before, the technology revolution is leading to government control of much of your lives where only a minority of government officials and employees will, either directly or indirectly, supervise and control your lives via a vast bureaucracy of laws and regulations. Don't forget that more crime follows more laws and regulations and not the other way around. Corruption, extortion, spying and many other abuses of power, the acquisition of wealth in various ways, increased recognition and self-interest will follow and, in fact, is already happening. Altruism would take a back seat. Today, Russia, China and many other countries where power is centralized are characterized by all of the aforementioned in a variety of ways.

I can't resist telling you about one of my favorite spy stories. For reasons of confidentiality, I cannot mention the name of the spy whom I helped. It was in the '70s when an elderly man, through a friend of mine, arranged to meet me to discuss a vaccine that he had developed to treat cancer of the uterine cervix. I forget how it happened but he arranged for a clinical study in Mexico to test his theory but ran out of money to continue it. What is interesting is that he was the son of one of the wealthiest U.S. entrepreneurs who passed away but had married a much younger woman, younger than my friend, who inherited all of his money. When he asked her for more money to continue with his research, she refused. He asked me if I would go to Mexico and review the clinical data though he couldn't pay for my expenses. For some reason I concluded that he was a brilliant man and decided to go to Mexico, pay my way and review the data. I was impressed by the data, but that's another story. It's a long fascinating story which I have written about elsewhere, one influential player in my Doctornaut effort. One night, after a couple of drinks, he told me he was also a spy for our government, which almost floored me.

And here's the story: the communist Soviet Union had erected the Iron Wall after World War II, and it was virtually impossible to obtain information about certain things, one being the facts about the structure and population of Russia's capitol, Moscow. For reasons that have escaped my memory bank, he had access to travel to Moscow. Though you may think this is not a big thing, nylon stockings for women had just been invented. Women went crazy over them. He took a bunch of them to Moscow and made a deal with the secretary of a high-level Soviet official. He would give her the stockings in exchange for a Moscow telephone book which revealed much about the city. She readily agreed, and my friend gave it to the U.S. government.

Here's another story regarding spying, the nature of which is going on big-time in our country. Before WWII erupted, Hitler sent students and young athletes to Great Britain as an apparent gesture of good will. Little did the Brits know that a number of them were spies. For example, after the war a detailed map of London was discovered in German documents that enhanced their bombing efficacy of London during the war. Currently, we have thousands of foreign students in our universities and others working in our corporations. This is something to seriously think about. Have you ever?

Getting back to the subject matter, I don't want you to get the wrong impression regarding laws and regulations. They are essential. Just imagine that if tomorrow all laws and regulations in our country were immediately nullified. National chaos and destruction would follow the day after tomorrow, including looting and killings among many other catastrophic happenings. Just think about it for a moment.

Before I forget, one secret of life is *dosing.* For example, we deal with how much to eat, drink, work and take care of others among many other aspects of our existence. The same holds for how much power government should have. Too little–chaos; too much–tyranny; compromise–our country; just right–heaven.

Now don't think that networking is a shady or devious method, though it sometimes can be, to get what you want. It's a natural, self-preservation or self-interest trait of the human mind. You do it all the time with your family, friends and others. How many times have you networked with your mother to convince your father to fulfill your wishes–and vice versa? Though I won't squeal about the details, how many times have you networked with me to persuade your parents to have it your way?

You should know that the success of my long career has largely been due to networking with highly influential people, some of whom even became my friends. The belief that one shouldn't do business with your friends is pure baloney. They helped me reach the highest levels of various types of powerful leaders be it in our country or international ones. And there's what I call pyramiding, where one connection leads to many more. And, oftentimes, there's excitement and even pleasure when networking with others.

Don't forget that the largest networking group, perhaps in the world, are the lobbyist organizations in Washington D.C. Corporations, foundations, public policy groups, teachers, labor unions and foreign countries, among many others, contribute large sums of money to influence members of Congress and other high level groups to fulfill their objectives.

I want to more than strongly urge you to develop your networking skills now because they are critical for you to adapt to the already oncoming of pervasive government control and particularly the need to connect with its agents as well as those connected to them for they all are on their way.

And now, before signing off, some practical advice regarding the breadth and depth of your minds which is also applicable to certain others of your age range: Olivia, you have an admirable gift of a broad and voracious thirst for knowledge, which far exceeds that which I had. I'm impressed.

Stephen Carlos, you have a different gift in your exceptional ability to analyze a total situation.

Olivia, let's first start out with you for in the traditional world a common saying, as a sign of respect for women, was "ladies first." For you I would recommend that you concentrate on developing your skills of analysis in order to better assess what's going on in the world instead of absorbing and depending on the myriad messages of the Internet Democracy and other informational inputs. I would select one specific subject to objectively and deeply analyze. It's also an effective way to get rid of emotional and stubborn hang-ups and beliefs which are now everywhere. It's in the nature of the human mind to embrace comfortable stubbornness of one's beliefs rather than challenge them and confront one of life's greatest difficulties, to change one's mind.

I was your age when I first had an intense, deep analytical experience on the pro and con arguments regarding the existence of God as well as the claims of Christianity in the Bible. It made me a more honest and capable intellect, in general.

As far as you're concerned, I would ponder what subject matter that interests you the most and maybe, after discussing this with trusted others, move forward and get it done. Just take my word for it; it will open up important doors of life that you currently don't see.

Stephen Carlos, and now to you: I would strongly urge you to further develop your communication skills, coupled with broadening your base of knowledge. I have been impressed by your analytical skills and by your impressive ability to occasionally express them. You must, however, make it a regular habit which will inevitably open further doors. When I was in junior high school, my black social studies teacher, Mrs. Jenkins, pushed me to run for president of the school which would require making a presentation in front of the entire school body. You have got to remember that it was at the time when I was about your age, living in an old Italian neighborhood and had never spoken in public. I was scared shit and decided to refuse her offer until Milton, the black student and good guy who sat next to me in class, persuaded me to take the risk.

The night before my speech, while lying on the living room floor, I wrote my speech down on paper–with a pencil, for I had no pen. For some reason, I didn't tell my parents about the opportunity. Well, I rattled through my presentation like a machine gun, and it was an unequivocal catastrophe. My opponent was experienced in public speaking and easily won the election.

Jumping ahead in time to when I was in medical school, I read about a night course on public speaking for businessmen offered by the dynamic Madame Emtage, who, I believe, also trained Bishop Fulton Sheen, then one of our great public speakers. For some reason, she took a personal liking to me and spent extra time trying to develop my skills. She began by developing my voice projection, and I used to hold my nose in the bathroom while speaking aloud while my mom and dad were downstairs wondering whether I was losing my mind. Well, thank God, she did a great job in giving me confidence which immensely helped my career.

Based on this personal experience and the current world of communication, I would strongly urge you to take a course in public speaking.

Before I sign off, it just jumped to mind about our conversation with all three of us at the *gelateria* regarding why people are the way they are. I didn't have the answer then, but now I do. It has to do with the frog and the scorpion.

There was a male frog sitting by the edge of a lake who heard the inviting mating call of his girlfriend from the other side. With hormones flowing, he was ready to jump into the water and swim to meet her. Just as he was about to dive in a nearby scorpion asked, "Mr. Frog, would you please carry me on your back to the other side of the lake?" The frog, dumbfounded, answered, "Mr. Scorpion, are you out of your damn mind? If you jump on my back, you'll sting me for my blood, and then I'll die!" The scorpion, a very clever arachnoid, answered, "Mr. Frog, are you nuts? If I sting you while we're in the water, you'll sink, and then we'll both die, for I can't swim." Surprised and persuaded by the scorpion's argument, the frog told him to hop on his back. Then halfway across the lake, the scorpion stung the frog. The frog, once more dumbfounded, cried out, "Mr. Scorpion, how can you do this for we're now both going to die?" The scorpion, somewhat confused himself, answered, "I'm truly sorry, Mr. Frog. *I just couldn't help it, for it's in my nature!*"

Well, my grandchildren, it's time to close down. We covered a lot of territory and hopefully this thin book will help you adapt to the rapid transition from the traditional world, which you only experienced a part of, into the technological one.

At age 85, I don't know how long I'll be around but, as of now, I'm only an hour away by car for words of wisdom and refuse to use Zoom. And remember—always stick together!

Love and Sempre avanti,
Grandpa

P.S. After both of you read this book, let's get together and seriously discuss where you want to be ten years from now!

Your great grandparents, Anna and Stefano DeFelice

Your mother and father, Norma and Stephen DeFelice, when youthful romance bloomed

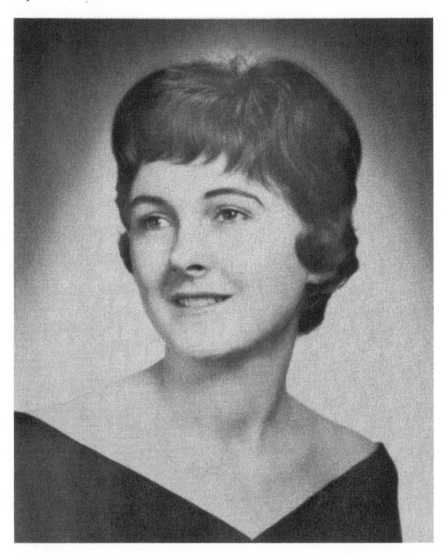

Your grandmother, Patrice DeFelice, President of her Class at Chestnut Hill College, Class of 1961

Your grandfather, Stephen DeFelice, President of Phi Alpha Sigma Fraternity at Jefferson Medical School, Class of 1961

Patrizia Park warmly kissing the great tenor, Luciano Pavarotti

Your cousin, **Maximilian Albrecht,** in his innocent youth with your great grandmother, **Agnes Kelly,** and family friend, **Bobby Thomson,** the legendary baseball player who hit baseball's most famous homerun, "the shot heard round the world."

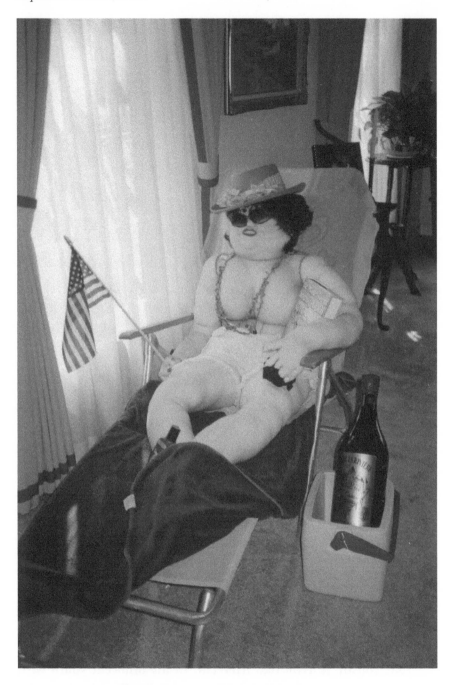

Naughty Aunt Ruth – remember her?

Lightning Source UK Ltd.
Milton Keynes UK
UKHW010247170621
385643UK00007B/319/J